CULTURES OF THE WORLD®

TAHITI

Roseline NgCheong-Lum

 **Marshall Cavendish**
Benchmark

New York

PICTURE CREDITS

Cover photo: © Dana Edmunds / Pacific Stock

age footstock / Bill Bachmann: 58 • age fotostock / Kevin O'Hara: 113 • age fotostock / Sylvain Grandadam: 45, 86, 112, 117 • age fotostock / Wojtek Buss: 48 • Audrius Tomonis: 135 • Bes Stock: 1, 5, 6, 7, 15, 16, 18, 27, 44, 63, 64, 65, 66, 76, 94, 104, 106, 109, 110, 120 • David Simson: 10, 36, 74, 87, 90, 93 • Focus Team: 72, 84, 97, 100, 101, 107, 123, 125 • Greenpeace Australia: 29, 38, 39 • HBL Network Photo Agency: 31, 32, 118 • Hoa Qui: 9, 12, 14, 21, 37, 41, 43, 60, 78, 95, 99, 116, 122, 127, 129 • Hulton Getty: 23, 25 • Hutchison Library: 111 • Jean-Bernard Carillet / Lonely Planet Images: 50, 126 • Life File: 47, 103 • Lonely Planet Images: 3, 53, 83 • Masterfile / Garry Black: 46, 57 • Mike Hosken: 70, 92, 105, 121 • Photobank: 17 • Photolibrary: 4, 13 • R. Ian Lloyd: 45, 48, 117 • Stockfood / Brauner, Michael: 131 • Stockfood / Foodphotogr. Eising: 130 • Tan Chung Lee: 28, 62, 81 • Tropix: 40

PRECEDING PAGE

Tahitian dancers performing a lively dance for tourists.

Publisher (U.S.): Michelle Bisson
Editors: Deborah Grahame, Mabelle Yeo, Sharon Low
Copyreader: Sherry Chiger
Designer: Jailani Basari
Cover picture researcher: Connie Gardner
Picture researcher: Thomas Khoo

Marshall Cavendish Benchmark
99 White Plains Road
Tarrytown, NY 10591
Web site: www.marshallcavendish.us

Originated and designed by Times Editions Private Limited
An imprint of Marshall Cavendish International (Asia) Private Limited
A member of Times Publishing Limited

All Internet sites were correct and accurate at the time of printing. All monetary figures in this publication are in U.S. dollars.

Library of Congress Cataloging-in-Publication Data
NgCheong-Lum, Roseline, 1962–
   Tahiti / by Roseline NgCheong-Lum. — 2nd ed.
     p. cm. — (Cultures of the world)
   Summary: "Provides comprehensive information on the geography, history, wildlife, governmental structure, economy, cultural
     diversity, peoples, religion, and culture of Tahiti"—Provided by publisher.
   Includes bibliographical references and index.
    ISBN 978-0-7614-2089-7
   1. Tahiti—Juvenile literature. I. Title.
   DU870.N49 2007
   996.2'11—dc22   2007014901

Printed in China

987654321

919.6211
2008

CONTENTS

INTRODUCTION   5

GEOGRAPHY   7
The island of Tahiti • Peaks and rivers • Papeete • Climate
• Flora • Fauna

HISTORY   19
Polynesian ancestors • Tahiti before the Europeans
• European discovery • Missionaries and colonial politics
• The French–Tahitian War • Établissements Français de l'Océanie
• Internal autonomy • Voices for independence

GOVERNMENT   33
The assembly • France and Tahiti • Local government • Nuclear
testing in the Pacific

ECONOMY   41
Government spending • Agriculture • Trade • Tourism
• Fishing • Le truck

ENVIRONMENT   51
Forests • Marine environment • Effects of nuclear testing
• Waste management

TAHITIANS   59
Polynesians • Demis • Chinese • Popaa • Tahitian dress

LIFESTYLE   67
Class structure • The Tahitian house • Health care • Education
• Social problems • Vahine

A hawksbill turtle swimming over coral reefs in the Tuamoto Channel.

RELIGION   77
The Evangelical Church • The Catholic Church • Other churches
• Polynesian faith

LANGUAGE   87
The Tahitian language • French • Newspapers • Radio and television

ARTS   95
Dancing • Painting • Literature • Carving

LEISURE   105
Music • The lure of water • Sports • Gambling • Bringue

FESTIVALS   113
Heiva i Tahiti • Bastille Day • Religious festivals • Fairs
• Chinese New Year

FOOD   121
Fish • All-purpose trees • Staples • The Tahitian oven
• Tahitian drinks • Papeete market

MAP OF TAHITI   132

ABOUT THE ECONOMY   135

ABOUT THE CULTURE   137

TIME LINE   138

GLOSSARY   140

FURTHER INFORMATION   141

BIBLIOGRAPHY   142

INDEX   142

A Tahitian girl with her garland and wreath of fresh tropical flowers.

INTRODUCTION

NESTLED IN THE HEART of the Pacific Ocean, Tahiti is a land of dramatic contrasts. Tall, craggy mountains frame beaches of white sand lapped by gentle waves. Papeete, the capital, is cosmopolitan and bustling with activity, while the peninsula that makes up the eastern part of the island remains wild and undeveloped.

Beyond the postcard images of luxurious holidays are a people who have to confront the common struggles of modern living, such as rising unemployment, crime, and pollution. Just like people elsewhere in the world, Tahitians face the multiple problems of a rapidly changing world. Tahiti is blessed with beautiful beaches and a unique marine environment. The challenge for the Tahitian people is to preserve this beauty while effectively utilizing their resources to the optimum. Above all, they need to find a way to reconcile their Polynesian heritage with their contemporary political status as a French territory.

GEOGRAPHY

THE ISLAND OF TAHITI in the Pacific Ocean forms part of the "Polynesian triangle," which includes Hawaii in the north, Easter Island in the east, and New Zealand in the southwest.

French Polynesia is spread over a total area of 1,545,007 square miles (4,001,550 square km), about half of the size of the U.S. mainland. It is made up of 118 islands, which have a combined land area of only 1,609 square miles (4,167 square km). These islands are divided into five archipelagoes: the Society Islands, the Austral Islands, the Tuamotu Islands, the Gambier Islands, and the Marquesas Islands. The Society Islands are further divided into the Windward Islands and the Leeward Islands. Located in the Windward group, the largest island in French Polynesia is Tahiti, where most of the population lives. Tahiti is also the commercial, cultural, and social center of French Polynesia. Other important islands are Moorea, Huahine, and Raiatea.

THE ISLAND OF TAHITI

Although Tahiti is the largest island in French Polynesia, it is only about one-third of the size of Rhode Island. However, its area of 402 square miles (1,041 square km) accounts for about one-quarter of the total land area of French Polynesia. It is also the highest island, with its tallest mountain reaching 7,333 feet (2,235 m).

The islands of French Polynesia are of two types: volcanic islands, also called high islands, and coral islands, also called atolls. Tahiti is a high island ringed by a coral reef. It is shaped like an hourglass lying more or

Above: **The pristine waters of Tuherera beach and the abundant vegetation of the village of Tikehau provide a captivating picture of idyllic natural beauty.**

Opposite: **Lush tropical vegetation and beautiful waterfalls characterize Tahiti's mountainous interior.**

The word Polynesia *is made up of two Greek words,* poly *and* nesos, *which mean "many islands."*

less horizontal. The larger section of the hourglass, Tahiti Nui (Big Tahiti), takes up the western side of the island. Papeete, the capital, is located on the northwest coast of Tahiti Nui. Most commercial and leisure activity is concentrated in the town and the area surrounding it. The airport of Faaa is about 4 miles (6.4 km) from Papeete.

The smaller part of Tahiti is a peninsula called Tahiti Iti (Small Tahiti) or Taiarapu. It is mostly undeveloped, and there is no road going all the way around it. The narrow neck of the hourglass is called Taravao, and it acts as a refueling center for people traveling around Tahiti. Taravao is also a dynamic town with schools, businesses, and cultural activities. Bridging Tahiti Nui and Tahiti Iti, it is larger and more developed than the neighboring districts.

Like Hawaii's Maui, Tahiti was formed by two ancient volcanoes, which joined at the isthmus of Taravao. The centers of both parts of Tahiti are mountainous and craggy. Steep slopes crossed by deep ravines descend to the coastal plain. Waterfalls are a common sight; Vaimahuta, near Tiarei in the northeast, is one of the most beautiful. Rainbows form above the waterfalls as the sun's rays filter through the droplets of water. In fact, there is a phrase, *Tahiti-nui-te-vai-uri-rau*, which means "Great Tahiti of the many-colored waters."

The coastal plain varies in width from a few feet (around 1 m) to more than a mile (1.6 km) at its widest in the north at Pirae and the south at Papara. Only the coastal plain is inhabited.

The northeastern coast is rugged and rocky because there is no barrier reef. Waves ride in high, pounding the shore with great intensity. Villages lie in a narrow strip between the mountains and the ocean. The Pari Coast, at the southeastern tip of the peninsula, has spectacular cliffs with a drop of nearly 1,000 feet (305 m) down to the ocean. The southern

BIRTH OF AN ATOLL

Islands in the ocean are formed by underwater volcanic eruptions. As the volcano explodes, magma is pushed up above sea level, and an island emerges. At first it is shaped like a cone. After the mass has cooled down, rains erode the land over time, and valleys and mountains are carved out of the cone. Once this phase is over, the polyps (a type of microorganism) present in the sea start to form a reef, and the island gradually becomes surrounded by a ring of coral.

Over several million years, as the rains cause the island to slowly erode away, the coral reef grows higher and higher, rising to about 3–7 feet (0.9–2.1 m) above sea level. Vegetation starts to grow on this ring, and the edges become beaches. As the ring is not of the same height throughout, the parts that jut out of the sea become coral islands. These are called *motu* (moh-TOO) in Tahitian. When the last volcanic peak of the first island is completely submerged by the sea, leaving only the ring of coral islands surrounding a lagoon, an atoll is born.

"Closed" atolls have no break in the reef. The only way water is exchanged between the ocean and the lagoon is through shallow channels called *hoa* (HOH-ah) in Tahitian. "Open" atolls can have one or more breaks in the reef, promoting a greater exchange of water and marine species between the ocean and the lagoon. Makatea, in the Tuamotu archipelago, is the only "raised" atoll in French Polynesia. The reef that turned into the island was wider and higher, thus forming a plateau with no lagoon.

Tahiti's steep mountains and valleys are very scenic, but they make the interior of the island unsuitable for habitation and agriculture.

coast, on the other hand, is protected by a reef, and its sandy beaches are gently lapped by the waves. The coastal plain is broad and supports large gardens and coconut groves. All around Tahiti, the depth of the lagoon between the reef and the island varies from 25 feet (7.6 m) to 100 feet (30.5 m).

The coastline is cut here and there by deep bays. Matavai Bay is where most of the early explorers landed. All ships moored in Matavai Bay until the 1820s, when the better-protected harbor of Papeete became more popular.

PEAKS AND RIVERS

The centers of Tahiti Nui and Tahiti Iti are made up of several tall peaks surrounding a deep depression. The depressions, called calderas, are the former craters of the volcanoes whose explosions led to the formation of the island. The tallest mountain on Tahiti Nui is Mount Orohena. Its rounded summit rises up to 7,333 feet (2,235 m). Tahiti Iti's tallest peak is

Mount Roniu at 4,341 feet (1,323 m). Altogether there are eight mountains on the island of Tahiti. One of the most intriguing outcrops is Mount Diademe, a thin rectangular blade of basalt that rises to 3,960 feet (1,207 m).

There are more than 100 rivers and streams all over Tahiti. The longest river is Papenoo, which originates from the northern side of the caldera of Tahiti Nui. At its source, where it is spanned by the longest bridge in Tahiti, it is called Vaituoru. It then becomes Papenoo and flows 15 miles (24 km) through the Papenoo Valley down to the sea. On its way it is joined by several other rivers, finally dividing into two before reaching the sea. The widest and fastest-flowing river in Tahiti is the Vaitepiha on the peninsula.

PAPEETE

Tahiti's capital takes its name from the Papeete River, which used to flow nearby. Meaning "water basket," Papeete was nothing but swampland until Rev. James Crook, an English missionary, settled there in 1818. The missionaries of the London Missionary Society soon followed suit, and the town grew rapidly as a result. Its excellent harbor made it a place of trade and a favorite port of call for whalers. After Tahiti was made a French colony in 1880, Papeete became the seat of the governor.

The urban spread now extends over 25 miles (40 km), from Paea in the west to Mahina in the north. The outskirting districts of Papenoo and Papara are also slowly becoming urbanized. Even the island of Moorea has become almost a suburb of Papeete, now that there are regular air and sea links between the two neighbors.

With its modern harbor facilities and the only international airport to service French Polynesia—Faaa airport—Papeete is now a major stopover for shipping and flights across the Pacific. French Polynesia's exports are transported from Papeete port, and a power plant supplies electricity for the island.

Tahiti has only one lake, Lake Vaihiria, perched at an altitude of 1,500 feet (457 m). It is known for its huge eels endowed with large, earlike fins. According to legend, the first eel crawled across the mountains from a pool in Arue on the northern coast. Feeling lonely, the eel married a beautiful maiden. The present-day inhabitants are supposed to be the descendants of this incongruous couple.

Although it now stretches across the full length of Tahiti's northwest coast, Papeete grew up around its port, which is still the heart of the city.

The town center, with warehouses and branch offices of companies, faces the harbor. Most buildings are modern and two or three stories high. Government buildings and the courts of justice are located in the administrative sector. In contrast to the rest of the town, Vaiami Hospital and the naval regiment are still housed in beautiful colonial buildings. Around the administrative sector is the commercial section of town, with banks and offices. To the north lies Fare Ute industrial zone. The missionary quarter is south of the town center. Catholic and Protestant schools stand next to small houses.

The main street of Papeete is Boulevard Pomare, which curves around the harbor. It is lined with modern shopping malls, libraries, museums, and churches. The post office and the public swimming pool are also located there. In the heart of the waterfront area lies Bougainville Park, which is crowned by a massive banyan tree. This peaceful oasis features running streams and lush vegetation.

Beyond the town center is a motley collection of slums, middle-income houses, businesses, and industrial zones. Six of Tahiti's 21 communes (administrative districts) are adjacent to Papeete and relatively urban: Paea, Punaauia, Faaa, Pirae, Arue, and Mahina. The lower-income groups can be found in Faaa, Paea, and the western side of Mahina. The higher grounds of Pirae and Punaauia are reserved for the beautiful houses of more affluent residents.

The urban area in and around Papeete is home to more than 127,000 inhabitants, accounting for about 65 percent of the population of French Polynesia. The population of Papeete is still growing as more islanders leave their native villages to look for work in the capital. The corollary of this fast-paced growth is increasing problems of air, water, and noise pollution.

CLIMATE

Because Tahiti lies in the tropics, the climate is warm almost all year round. There are roughly two seasons: hot and rainy from November to April, with average temperatures ranging from 72°F to 90°F (22–32°C), and relatively cool and dry from May to October, with temperatures between 64°F and 72°F (18–22°C). At high altitudes, the temperature is much lower; in the cool season, nighttime temperatures on Mount Orohena can even drop to freezing.

The climate of Tahiti is tempered by cooling breezes from the sea. In the hot season, the prevailing winds are the northeast trade winds. In the cool season, it is the strong southeast trade wind, called *maraamu* (mah-rah-AH-moo), that dominates. A mountain wind called *hupe* (HOO-pay) blows down onto the coastal plains in the evening. Rainfall is erratic, with Papeete recording an average of

Strong winds along the coast of Tahiti. The French Polynesian region experiences heavy rain and thunderstorms from December to March.

13

73 inches (185 cm) yearly. The northeast trade winds bring the most rain, and Papenoo, in the northeast, receives twice as much rain as Punaauia on the western coast. Devastating floods are frequent in the Papenoo Valley during the rainy season. The mountainous region in the center of the island also receives much rain. Most rain falls from December to March. Humidity is high throughout the year, reaching 98 percent during the hotter months. Tahiti also faces cyclones, which occur from January to March. Cyclone Veena in 1983 registered winds of up to 140 miles (225 km) per hour and is still remembered by Tahitians for the damage it caused.

The sweet-smelling *tiare* is Tahiti's national flower. A festival is held in its honor in December.

FLORA

Tahiti used to be covered with forests of hibiscus, casuarina, rosewood, and chestnut. Along the coast, only a few pockets of these plants remain today, although wild hibiscus is still quite common on higher ground.

The plant life of Tahiti varies according to the altitude. Along the coast, aside from the pockets of forest, a variety of tropical trees grow in profusion, including coconut palms, pandanus, and almond trees. The hillsides and valleys support fruit trees such as guava, mango, lime, grapefruit, and orange. Other fruits that are planted on a large scale are pineapples, papaya, and bananas. Vanilla and coffee grow in the valleys and on the plateaus. Flowering trees include lantana, acacia, and ylang-ylang. One interesting feature of Tahitian flora is that there are no plants with thorns aside from raspberry plants and another common plant that lies flat and is easily recognized. As a result, Tahitians can walk barefoot without getting injured.

On the slopes from 1,500 feet to 2,700 feet (457–823 m) high, the vegetation consists mainly of a few trees and ferns that grow in dense clumps. Farther up, forests of hardwood trees reappear. They are called "the forest of clouds," and because of the high humidity, tree trunks are covered with epiphytes and other creepers. The strong winds blow the trunks into strange, tortuous shapes.

Tahiti's national flower is the *tiare Tahiti*, from the gardenia family. The small, white, sweet-smelling flower is used to make headdresses and garlands or simply worn behind the ear. Tahitians have a long-standing love affair with flowers. Roads are lined with hibiscus, frangipani, bougainvillea, and flame of the forest, and even the humblest house is decorated with bright flowers.

The stunning coral reefs and clear blue water of the Tikehau Lagoon.

*Next to Matavai
Bay is Point Venus,
so named because
Captain James
Cook observed the
transit of the planet
Venus across the
sun from this point
in 1769.*

A noddy, one of the many
species of birds in Tahiti.
It lives on small fish and
other marine life that it
procures from the surface
of the open seas beyond
the reefs.

FAUNA

Land fauna in Tahiti is rather scarce. Many of the animals on the island were introduced by the first Polynesians to come to the islands. The wild pig, with a mane at the neck, a long snout, tusks, and long legs, was the first animal to be brought into Tahiti. It has become a rarity due to hunting, so it is protected from extinction by a law regulating the number of wild pigs that can be killed. Wild chickens exist in the coastal regions, and herds of wild goats roam the plateaus of Fautaua and Tuauru. The early Polynesians also brought dogs, rats, and lizards stowed away on their canoes. Europeans introduced domestic animals such as horses, cows, and cats.

Several types of fish are found in the rivers of Tahiti, including eels, jacks, sleepers, *kemeridae*, gobies, mullet, and *syngnathidae*. The most abundant are the eels, of which there are three species. Eared eels, however, have almost disappeared from Tahiti's rivers. In addition, there are four species of freshwater shrimps, a few mollusks, and some insects. The *tupa* is a land crab that digs holes and tunnels near the lagoon. There are also a number of snails, and the tiny *partula* is used for making necklaces.

The waters off the coast of Tahiti are richer in animal life. Seven hundred species of fish inhabit the lagoon, and sharks and reptiles can be found beyond the reef. Tropical fish are colorful, and some, like the grouper, can grow to substantial dimensions. Green turtles and hawksbill turtles are quite common. On rare occasions, sea snakes can be found in the water.

There are about 90 species of birds in Tahiti, most of them indigenous to French Polynesia. One of the most impressive is the tropic bird, with its two long, red tail feathers. These feathers were prized as royal emblems in ancient Tahiti. Of the land birds, the Tahitian swallow is one of the most common.

Few insects in Tahiti are seriously harmful to people, except for the mosquito, which carries diseases such as filariasis and dengue fever, and the millipede, whose "bite" can be dangerous to infants and the elderly.

Turtles thrive in Polynesia's warm tropical waters.

HISTORY

FOR A LONG TIME the people of Tahiti led a serene life isolated from, and unknown to, the rest of the world. They had no writing system and did not work with metal—in fact, they did not work at all, at least not as the Europeans knew work. Apart from a few hours of fishing or collecting food, they spent most of the day engaged in leisure activities.

However, almost from the moment the island was discovered by European explorers, it attracted visitors lured by the myths of the "noble savage" and paradise on earth. European colonization and the introduction of "civilization" brought diseases and evils that did not exist there previously. The lifestyle on Tahiti was irremediably changed.

Tahiti was always described by those who visited the island in terms of what they themselves felt or perceived, never through the eyes of the local population. Even today, its rich "prediscovery" history is overshadowed by the events related to the appearance of the first European explorers. Tahitians are still perceived as a gentle people leading an idyllic lifestyle. The reality is that of a subjugated people who have long demanded political independence. Although Tahitians now enjoy a greater degree

Opposite: **These sculptures tell of the culture of the ancient Polynesian natives.**

A POLYNESIAN "NOBLE SAVAGE"

After Captain James Cook's second voyage to Tahiti, a young man named Omai, from the island of Raiatea, boarded Cook's ship and sailed to England with the expedition. Omai acted as translator on the other islands they visited and was greeted with much interest upon his arrival in England. European romantic literature of the 18th century glorified the concept of the "noble savage," who symbolized goodness untouched by civilization. Omai, who seemed to be the typical "noble savage," was presented to the king and introduced to the prominent members of English society. He attended balls and parties and even inspired a few successful plays. Omai returned to Tahiti with Cook in 1777, but his long absence made him feel alienated from his own people.

of autonomy under the French government and more control over many aspects of daily life, they still do not have complete sovereignty over their destiny.

POLYNESIAN ANCESTORS

The first people to settle in Polynesia came from Southeast Asia. Traveling east, they settled in Fiji around 1500 B.C., then in Tonga and Samoa a few centuries later. From these islands, they set sail for what is now French Polynesia around A.D. 300, settling first in the Marquesas. During the next 1,000 years they settled in Easter Island, Hawaii, the Society Islands, and New Zealand.

Overpopulation on one island led the Polynesians to set off in search of new islands. The first step was to make a voyage of exploration for suitable islands. Once a sufficiently large island was found, the explorers noted its direction in relation to the stars and returned home to fetch their families, animals, and plants so as to establish settlements on the new island.

The ancient Polynesians were skilled navigators. They traveled in large double-hulled canoes, using the position of the sun and the stars to direct them. They were also able to anticipate the appearance and proximity of land by noting changes in the waves.

In 1976 the *Hokulea*, an oceangoing canoe built from ancient designs, sailed from Hawaii to Tahiti using only traditional navigational techniques based on the stars and the swells of waves. This voyage proved beyond doubt that the ancient Polynesians were some of the greatest sailors of all time.

By sailing a raft called *Kon-Tiki* from Peru to islands east of Tahiti in 1947, Swedish explorer Thor Heyerdahl tried to prove that the Polynesians could have come from South America. This theory has largely been debunked as a result of archaeological findings. However, it is almost certain that there was some form of contact, as the sweet potato, which originated in South America, can be found in Polynesia, even if corn—the staple food of South America—does not exist in Polynesia. It is believed that if South Americans had gone on to colonize the islands, they would certainly have brought their staple food along.

TAHITI BEFORE THE EUROPEANS

Ancient Tahitian society was highly hierarchical. There were three distinct classes: *arii* (ah-REE-ee), or high chiefs; *raatira* (rah-AH-tee-rah), or minor chiefs and landowners; and *manahune* (mah-nah-HOO-nay), or

Although the ancient Polynesian society is gone forever, modern Tahitians perform historical reenactments as part of their festivals.

common people. People from the different classes did not mix with each other, and children born of the union between a chief and a commoner were killed. Men and women were segregated most of the time, especially at mealtimes, and women were not allowed to participate in religious ceremonies.

The *arii* had absolute authority over their subjects, who considered the *arii* almost godlike. The *arii* had to be physically higher than everyone else and were carried everywhere by their subjects. When they stood, their subjects had to sit down; when they were seated, the latter had to lie down.

The *manahune* were servants, farmers, and fishermen. They could not move out of their class unless they became priests or warriors. Between the chiefs and the commoners were the landowners. The landowners

LOVE FOR A NAIL

The crew of the *Dolphin* discovered that Tahitians desired nails more than the usual offerings of beads, knives, and mirrors. The Tahitians would give enormous quantities of fruits, pigs, and chickens in return for a nail. The reason was simple: Metal nails could easily be bent into fishhooks, which had previously been carved with much effort from mother-of-pearl.

In return for sexual favors, Tahitian women would request nails from the sailors. As more and more of the *Dolphin*'s crew went ashore to meet women, the ship's master became concerned about where all the nails were coming from. The carpenter assured him that the ship's stock of nails was under lock and key. However, when they proceeded to check the ship, they found that nails had been pulled out of the woodwork. And they soon discovered that two-thirds of the crew were sleeping on the deck because the nails on which their hammocks were slung had disappeared. The ship's officers had to take swift action before the whole ship fell to pieces. One sailor was punished as a scapegoat, and the other crew members were warned that they would face dire punishment if caught going ashore with a nail.

owed the same respect to the chiefs as the *manahune*, and their authority was limited to relaying orders from the chiefs to the commoners and seeing that they were carried out.

Tahiti was divided into several districts, each ruled by an *arii*. Wars frequently broke out between the tribes, and the vanquished were often taken as slaves by the victors.

EUROPEAN DISCOVERY

On June 17, 1767, Captain Samuel Wallis chanced upon the island of Tahiti during an exploratory trip in search of the southern landmass that was thought to balance the northern hemisphere. He anchored his ship, the HMS *Dolphin*, at Taiarapu in the southern part of the island. The next day he sailed farther north looking for a more pleasant anchorage and landed in Matavai Bay. Hundreds of canoes surrounded the ship, and the islanders seemed friendly at first. However, they then started pelting the crew with stones, and the Englishmen opened fire with their cannons. On June 24, Wallis took formal possession of the island for the British crown and called it King George III's Island. After a few more rounds of cannon firing, the Tahitians decided to cooperate with the invaders and supplied them with fresh water and food. The *Dolphin* left Tahiti after a few weeks, but news of the discovery did not reach England until a year later.

Two French ships, the *Etoile* and the *Boudeuse*, under the command of Louis-Antoine de Bougainville, arrived in Tahiti in April 1768. Unaware

Captain James Cook was the greatest of the Pacific maritime explorers. He recorded the lifestyle and customs of the Tahitians and took a real interest in their culture. After his first visit to Tahiti, he sailed west and became the first European to chart the coasts of New Zealand and eastern Australia.

"The scene we saw was the truest picture of Arcadia, of which we were going to be kings, that the imagination can form."

—Joseph Banks, English botanist who visited Tahiti in 1769

of the visit of Wallis and the English claim to the island, Bougainville claimed Tahiti for France, giving it the name of New Cythera, in reference to the birthplace of the Greek goddess of love, Aphrodite. Back in France, he promoted the idea of an idyllic land where a gentle people lived on the bounty of the land and the sea, free from the restrictions of European life. Bougainville's recollections of Tahiti were published in 1771 in a book entitled *Voyage autour du monde.* The book was a resounding success and disseminated the myth of the island paradise.

The third European associated with Tahiti was the English explorer Captain James Cook, who visited the island four times between 1769 and 1777. During his first visit, he stayed three months to observe the transit of the planet Venus across the sun. He traveled around the whole island and drew a precise map of Tahiti. With him were two botanists, Joseph Banks and Daniel Solander, who collected an enormous number of species of plants, birds, fish, and insects, which added greatly to the scientific knowledge of the time. Cook's subsequent voyages enabled him to give the world greater details of Polynesian society.

At the time of Tahiti's discovery by Europeans, the local population numbered around 150,000. The Europeans brought diseases to which the Tahitians had no immunity: syphilis, tuberculosis, smallpox, and dysentery. By 1865 only 7,169 inhabitants remained.

MISSIONARIES AND COLONIAL POLITICS

Thirty years after the island was discovered by Europeans, a shipload of missionaries from the London Missionary Society arrived in Tahiti to convert the "heathens" from their "idolatrous ways." It took them 15 years to make their first convert, King Pomare II, who realized that the missionaries could be very useful to his rule and that British

MUTINY ON THE *BOUNTY*

In 1788 Lieutenant William Bligh came to Tahiti on board the HMS *Bounty* to collect young breadfruit trees to take to the West Indies. Bligh and his crew lived among the Tahitians for five months, and it was with reluctance that his crew subsequently set sail for Jamaica. Partly due to Bligh's severe treatment of the crew, many men supported crewman Fletcher Christian when he masterminded a mutiny to get rid of the ship's commander and return to blissful Polynesia. Bligh was abandoned on the open sea with 18 loyal men and some basic supplies. In one of the most impressive open-boat journeys in history, Bligh subsequently sailed 3,600 miles (5,794 km) to the Dutch Indies (Indonesia), suffering only one casualty on the way.

The mutineers first tried to settle on the Austral Islands but had to withdraw to Tahiti in the face of the inhabitants' hostility. Sixteen of them decided to stay in Tahiti. Christian, the rest of the crew, and a group of Tahitians sailed the *Bounty* to the uninhabited island of Pitcairn, where they burned the ship and founded the island's first settlement. The mutineers who settled in Tahiti were recaptured by a contingent on the HMS *Pandora* less than two years later. Four drowned in a shipwreck on the return trip, and the survivors were court-martialed in England. Three of the men were hanged.

The *Bounty* drama inspired three movies, made in 1935, 1962, and 1984.

commerce was important for the island. The Pomare clan had gained access to firearms through their association with the European explorers, enabling them to gain supremacy over the whole island and to establish Pomare I as the first king of Tahiti in 1790. After the conversion of Pomare II in 1812, all the other Tahitians followed suit, and the ancient Polynesian religion disappeared forever.

For nearly 40 years the Protestant missionaries enjoyed tremendous success in Tahiti. When Catholic missionaries arrived in 1835 with the intention of establishing their own mission (having failed in a brief attempt in 1774), the Protestants used their influence over the reigning monarch, Queen Pomare IV, to send them away.

In 1837 George Pritchard, a Protestant missionary, became the English consul. He encouraged Queen Pomare to ask the British to make Tahiti a protectorate of the English crown. In 1842 French admiral Abel Dupetit-Thouars arrived in Tahiti during the absence of both the English consul and the queen. With the help of the French consul, he organized the pro-French district chiefs to sign a demand for French protection. The French began to install themselves very firmly on the island, and after a series of threats Queen Pomare was forced to ratify the demand for a protectorate. On September 9, 1842, Tahiti was proclaimed a French protectorate. A government was established that consisted of the royal commissioner, a military governor, and the captain of the port of Papeete.

THE FRENCH-TAHITIAN WAR

After Tahiti officially became a protectorate of the French government, a protectorate flag was hoisted above Queen Pomare's palace, in place of her personal flag. Unhappy with this action, she protested to the king of France and looked to Britain for protection by taking refuge on

the HMS *Basilisk*, an English ship anchored in the Papeete harbor. This was the signal the population was waiting for; they immediately started a rebellion against the French invaders. Tahitian chiefs often took advantage of English and French disagreements by making alliances to further their own political aspirations and power struggles. To this end, the powerful rival chief Tati of Papara sided with the French in the hopes of gaining influence and overthrowing Pomare.

The first skirmishes took place in Taravao in March 1844. The following month, Governor Armand-Joseph Bruat engaged 400 men to carry out a bloody battle on Mahaena beach. The Tahitians lost 102 men and retreated to the Punaruu and Papenoo Valleys to carry out guerrilla attacks on the French forces. The fighting spread to the other islands, and the Polynesians experienced some success in January 1846 in Huahine, prompting them to attack Papeete, where they were defeated. The French-Tahitian War

A church in Arue. Roman Catholic missionaries had little success in Tahiti until the region became a French protectorate.

27

lasted nearly three years, ending when the French troops launched a decisive attack on Fautaua fort in December 1846. Queen Pomare agreed to accept the protectorate over Tahiti and Moorea on January 7, 1847.

ÉTABLISSEMENTS FRANÇAIS DE L'OCÉANIE

At the time of the protectorate, the central structure of Tahitian administration was composed of the royal court, the assembly, and the district councils. French authority was represented by the governor, assisted by various officers and civil servants. In 1866 the Tahitian legislative assembly voted for the introduction of French legislation, as proposed by the governor. When Pomare V abdicated in June 1880, all his territories were given to France in return for a pension of 5,000 francs a month, and Tahiti became a full-fledged French colony. In 1885 Tahiti and the other islands in the archipelago became the Établissements Français de l'Océanie (French Oceania).

This period was marked by the arrival of the French and other colonizers. The French settlers were mainly soldiers and sailors who decided to stay on after demobilization. Having no income of their own, they tried their hand at agriculture, cultivating the lands of their Tahitian wives without much success. The English, the Americans, and the Germans were more successful because they came from a wealthier background. Those who married into the local aristocracy gained access to much land and capital.

Many of the early Chinese immigrants returned to China when the cotton industry failed. Those who stayed went into business, setting up small grocery stores in rural areas. This Chinese-owned store is on the island of Bora Bora.

Expressing their anger and dissatisfaction with French rule, Tahitians rioted in Papeete after the resumption of French nuclear testing in 1995. Many Polynesians want complete independence from France.

Thus were started the wealthy families who still rule the world of commerce in Tahiti: the Salmons, the Laharragues, the Branders, and the Horts.

The Chinese were brought in as coolies to work in the cotton fields at Atimaono in the mid-1800s. Other immigrants came from Melanesia, the Gilbert Islands (now called Kiribati), Atiu, and Easter Island.

INTERNAL AUTONOMY

Tahiti was largely neglected by France at the beginning of the 20th century, and life there was harsh. Diseases and cyclones caused great destruction. However, with the opening of the Panama Canal in 1914, Tahiti became a port of call between Australia and the United States, and subsidies from the Colonial Office started to pour in. When World War I broke out, Tahiti sent a small contingent of volunteers for France.

After World War II, during which the Tahitian battalion earned honors at Bir Hakeim in North Africa, universal suffrage was granted to the Établissements Français de l'Océanie in 1945, and all residents of the colony were granted French citizenship. In 1947 a World War I volunteer, Pouvanaa a Oopa, created the Pouvanaa Committee to oppose the arrival of additional civil servants from France. From then on, there were more demands for autonomy in Tahiti. Thus, on July 27, 1957, the Établissements Français de l'Océanie changed from a colony to a territory and became known as French Polynesia. After General Charles de Gaulle came back to power in France in 1958, a referendum was held to allow Tahitians to decide whether they wanted to remain French. Nearly two-thirds of the electorate were in favor of the French commonwealth.

In 1963 France moved its nuclear program from Algeria (which had by then acquired independence) to French Polynesia. Subsequently the islands of Moruroa and Fangataufa were subjected to nearly 200 nuclear tests between 1966 and 1996. This program was to have wide-ranging repercussions on Tahitian society that are still being felt today, in ecological, health, and economic terms.

With the setting up of the Centre d'Expérimentation du Pacifique (CEP) and the arrival of its attendant problems, more and more voices started to make themselves heard for greater autonomy. In 1977 Tahiti was granted a new statute, giving the islanders slightly more say in its management. In 1984 full internal autonomy came into effect, and 20 years later, in 2004, the territory acquired more self-governing powers when it became an "overseas country," or *pays d'outre-mer*.

VOICES FOR INDEPENDENCE

With the election of Oscar Temaru to the French Polynesian presidency in 2004, French Polynesia had, for the first time in its history, a proindependence majority in parliament. The proindependence movement gained momentum after 1996 when, with the cessation of nuclear testing, the country's main source of income, the military, was suddenly cut off, resulting in widespread unemployment.

A former officer in the French navy, Temaru started his political career as an antinuclear activist. In May 2004, at the head of a five-party coalition, he was elected president of French Polynesia, only to be ousted in October of the same year by political maneuvering among his rivals. Following a popular outcry, by-elections were held in February 2005, and Temaru was reinstated as president in March 2005.

Although Temaru campaigned on a pro-independence platform, he also pledged that outright independence was not for the immediate future. In fact, only 20 percent of the local population favors full independence, although the majority of the parties in the governing coalition are pro-autonomy. The new government's program included an increase in minimum wages, workdays that do not start before 9 A.M., an improvement in social services, political decentralization, education reform, and a revision of the autonomy statute.

A Tahitian citizen exercises her right to vote in an election in Tahiti.

GOVERNMENT

UNLIKE THE OTHER FRENCH DEPENDENCIES, French Polynesia has the status of an overseas country, a designation it has enjoyed through the passing of the statutory law of February 27, 2004. This designation underlines the greater degree of autonomy the country now has. The assembly of French Polynesia is in charge of most of the government, with France's influence limited to providing subsidies, education, and security.

However, the constitution of France remains the supreme law of the land, and Tahitians do not have much control over several aspects of their government. Pro-independence movements have made appeals to the United Nations Special Committee of 24—which helps colonies achieve independence—to put the territory on the priority list of states awaiting decolonization.

Opposite: **A parliamentary session in Tahiti.**

THE ASSEMBLY

Tahiti, in common with the rest of French Polynesia, is governed by a territorial government made up of a president, a vice president, and 22 ministers, who are in charge of the daily running of the territory.

THE TAHITIAN FLAG

The Tahitian flag, composed of one horizontal white stripe between two red stripes, disappeared after the death of Pomare V, the last king of Tahiti. It was reinstated in 1975 alongside the French national flag. In 1984, when the territory attained internal autonomy, the French government recognized the Tahitians' right to determine the symbols expressing the personality of their nation, and this was how the current flag came about. A stylized canoe in red floating above a blue sea with yellow rays of sun at the back was added to the middle of the previous flag. Today this flag represents the whole of French Polynesia and is flown side by side with the French tricolor.

The president is elected by the assembly of French Polynesia, which also ratifies the president's choice of ministers.

Legislative power is in the hands of the 57 members of the assembly, who are elected for a period of five years. The territory is divided into districts, with 37 seats going to the Windward Islands (including Tahiti and Moorea), eight to the Leeward Islands, three to the Gambier Islands and the Tuamotu-East, three to the Tuamotu-West, three to the Austral Islands, and three to the Marquesas. Because of the electoral system, one vote in the Tuamotus has the weight of three in Tahiti. The assembly's primary function is to vote on the budget, but it can also dismiss the government through a motion of censure.

VOTING

Because Tahitians are granted full French citizenship, all persons aged 18 and older are allowed to take part in national as well as local elections. Tahitians vote for members of the Territorial Assembly and for their representatives in the French national assembly and senate. They also participate in elections for the European parliament. French civil servants and soldiers can vote in local elections (for the municipal councils and the Territorial Assembly) the day they arrive in the territory, and the conservative pro-French parties in the Territorial Assembly are propped up mainly by votes from French expatriates working in Tahiti.

At one time, it was the law that all men between the ages of 18 and 35—in Tahiti as in France—had to serve one year of active duty in the army, the navy, or the air force. Those who were not fit for military service had to serve two years of public service work or were deployed in other sectors of the government. In fact, many of the French civil servants in Tahiti used to be young Frenchmen in military service.

Outside of the two annual assembly sessions, a permanent commission is in place. In addition, the Economic and Social Committee brings together representatives from the various professions and establishes yearly reports.

FRANCE AND TAHITI

France is represented in the territory by a high commissioner. Assisted by a secretary-general, the high commissioner is in charge of the civil service, monetary policy, the national police, foreign affairs, immigration, defense, justice, and tertiary education. Despite the changes made by the statute of 2004, the high commissioner still wields considerable power and can dissolve the Territorial Assembly or refer its decisions to an administrative tribunal. The high commissioner can also impose a state of emergency if necessary.

French Polynesia is represented in Paris by two elected deputies in the French national assembly, a senator, and a social and economic councilor.

LOCAL GOVERNMENT

French Polynesia is divided into 48 communes, with 12 in Tahiti. The communes in the peninsula and the eastern half of Tahiti Nui are gathered into four groups of "associated communes." Each commune is managed by an elected municipal council, which chooses a mayor from its ranks. There are more than 900 municipal councilors throughout French Polynesia, elected by majority vote for a period of six years. The population size of each commune determines how many councilors it is entitled to elect.

French overseas departments and territories refer to France, particularly Paris, as the Métropole (usually translated as the "Mainland").

NATIONALISM

The first seeds of nationalism were sown by Pouvanaa a Oopa, an outspoken World War I hero from Huahine. In 1947 he founded the Pouvanaa Committee, which became the Rassemblement Démocratique des Populations Tahitiennes (Tahitian Democratic Group, or RDPT) in 1949. The RDPT was opposed to further deployment of French civil servants in Tahiti and wanted the country to move gradually toward independence. Pouvanaa's election to the French Chamber of Deputies in 1949 and to the vice presidency of the Government Council in 1957 afforded him a great opportunity to spread his separatist message among the population of Tahiti.

However, after he opposed General Charles de Gaulle during the constitutional referendum of 1958, Pouvanaa was arrested on trumped-up charges of arson, sentenced to jail, and exiled from Tahiti. Pouvanaa was not freed until 1968, well after the nuclear-testing facilities were established. In a powerful political comeback, he was elected to the French senate in 1971 and remained a senator until his death in 1977. Tahitians refer to him as *te metua*, "the father," as he is credited as being the father of Tahitian nationalism. His statue stands outside the Territorial Assembly.

Pouvanaa's legacy has been the creation of several pro-independence political parties. However, Tahitian politics is full of nuances. Most parties are nationalistic, but not all favor full independence. Those that actively call for immediate independence from France are the Polynesian Liberation Front, the Let the People Take the Power Party, and the Free Tahitians' Party. Most politicians, however, favor a more moderate form of independence, in which Tahiti could enjoy complete self-government without severing its ties with France.

Nationalism is strongest on the island of Tahiti and weakest in the Tuamotu Islands and the Marquesas, which are heavily dependent on French aid. Much of the rioting that took place in Papeete in September 1995 following France's resumption of nuclear testing in the Pacific was blamed on separatists trying to publicize their cause to the rest of the world. However, it is strategically important for France to maintain a colony in the Asia-Pacific region, where other countries still have military bases. Because France does not want to lose this foothold, it is unwilling to grant full independence to Tahiti or the rest of French Polynesia.

Local government

Each archipelago is run by an administrator, usually a French civil servant, appointed by the state. He or she has almost complete control over the elected municipal councils. The administrators of the Windward, Tuamotu-Gambier, and Austral Islands are based in Papeete.

Local government is responsible for public hygiene, social services, and energy. Since French Polynesia achieved internal autonomy it has also been responsible for the local police. One of the duties of the mayor is to solemnize marriages.

Papeete's town hall.

The distinctive shape of the mushroom cloud rises from Moruroa after a nuclear detonation.

NUCLEAR TESTING IN THE PACIFIC

Despite vocal protests from the local population, the Centre d'Expérimentation du Pacifique (CEP)—Center for Experimentation in the Pacific—was set up in 1963 on the atolls of Moruroa and Fangataufa, about 750 miles (1,207 km) from Tahiti. French military personnel were stationed in large numbers in Tahiti, and the French military presence is still strongly felt in the country. The CEP was headquartered at Pirae, just east of Papeete, with a major support base opposite the yacht club at Arue.

The first bomb was detonated at Moruroa on July 2, 1966. Initially nuclear testing took place in the atmosphere, but in 1974, after 44 atmospheric explosions and following strong international protests, the CEP decided to switch to underground tests. In total, more than 190 nuclear devices were detonated.

In 1995 newly elected French president Jacques Chirac unleashed a storm of protests worldwide when the French government announced that it would resume nuclear testing in French Polynesia after having unofficially discontinued testing for three years. Rioting broke out in Papeete, the passenger terminal at the Faaa airport was set on fire, and troops were called in from other territories to quell the unrest. Among the demonstrators were young unemployed Tahitians, supporters of Tahiti's independence, and antinuclear activists from various Pacific Rim countries. In the face of such strong sentiment, the French government reduced the number of devices to be detonated from eight to six and announced that those were the last tests. The program effectively ended in 1996.

One of the highest-profile incidents was the sinking of the *Rainbow Warrior* in 1985. The Greenpeace vessel was docked in Auckland harbor in New Zealand while on its way to French Polynesia with a flotilla of

"The French treated us like rubbish, like rats. Now, you see what happens."

—Roti Make, a Tahitian, on the antinuclear rioting in 1995

38

yachts to protest the nuclear program when it was sunk by a group of French secret agents who had infiltrated the organization. The sinking caused a major international scandal, and two agents were sentenced to prison by a New Zealand court. In 2005 it was revealed that the operation had been personally sanctioned by the highest authorities in France, including then-president François Mitterand himself.

From the French political point of view, nuclear testing was necessary to maintain France's position as a world political and military power. The authorities dismissed the fears of Pacific Rim nations and maintained that nuclear test sites in Russia are actually closer to Paris than Moruroa is to its nearest neighbor. The French government, however, has never allowed any proper study to be conducted on the test atolls, maintaining a ban on any outside investigations of the sites that had been rigorously enforced since 1966. Even today it strongly rejects any claims that its nuclear program caused any harm to the people of French Polynesia. The French defense ministry is still in charge of the two atolls.

Protests against French nuclear testing in the Pacific have gone beyond the borders of French Polynesia. These children in Rarotonga are among the many Polynesians who believe that if the French must test nuclear weapons, they should do so in their own country.

ECONOMY

WITH THE SETTING UP of the Centre d'Expérimentation du Pacifique (CEP) in the 1960s, Tahiti was suddenly thrust into the modern world of consumerism. Instead of cultivating their own crops and fishing for their food, Tahitians became wage earners and had to depend on others to supply their dietary needs. Thousands were employed by the CEP and other government bodies. With the end of nuclear testing in 1996, this source of income suddenly stopped, replaced by a yearly economic development transfer of 18 billion French Pacific francs (US$189.5 million). Known by its acronym of DGDE, this money is paid by France directly into the French Polynesian budget to compensate the country for the customs taxes that it no longer receives from imported material connected with the nuclear testing operations.

Inevitably, with economic activity becoming far more complex and subject to the vagaries of the global economy, unemployment continues to

Left: **Papeete port is the hub of the region's trade.**

Opposite: **A man stands behind his stall of fish— the day's catch. Fishing is a major industry in Tahiti.**

rise. Those who became jobless after 1996 have been joined by immigrants from the outer islands as well as by young Tahitians leaving school with few qualifications. These jobless or occasional workers account for the growing slums on the outskirts of Papeete.

Subsistence agriculture is practiced mainly in the smaller islands, while most residents of Tahiti lead an urban lifestyle, working in factories and offices and spending their free time shopping, watching movies, and having fun with their friends.

GOVERNMENT SPENDING

Tahiti is heavily dependent on French government spending. At the departure of the French military upon the closure of the CEP, the French government pledged to maintain financial aid for civil activities in Tahiti in order to support the territory in fundamentally transforming its economy. In 2004 French Polynesia received $1.42 billion from France, while its total government budget reached $1.74 billion, with a quarter of its expenditure devoted to investment.

All residents of Tahiti, including French expatriates, pay a "solidarity tax" in lieu of personal income tax. In 1998 the government embarked on a vast reform of the taxation system, with the introduction of value-added tax (VAT), the abolition of import duties, and the lowering of customs duties in accordance with World Trade Organization directives. With the presence of the highly paid and free-spending French civil servants, the cost of living in Tahiti is very high, and even with the help of unemployment and social-security benefits, many Tahitians find it difficult to make ends meet.

AGRICULTURE

Since much of Tahiti's interior is mountainous, very little land is devoted to agriculture. Agricultural activity takes place mainly in four areas: Papara commune, Teva I Uta commune, the isthmus and plateau of Taravao, and the east coast. With the use of modern technology, agriculture in these areas is practiced on an intensive basis. Even so, this sector now accounts for less than 5 percent of total output and employment.

Nearly half of the lowlands of Papara are under cultivation. The commune produces vegetables, flowers, pork, and poultry. The neighboring commune of Teva I Uta specializes in vegetable production and cattle rearing. Cattle are raised on coconut plantations, and the coconut plantations of Teva I Uta are the largest in Tahiti. However, many of the coconut trees are more than 100 years old, and Tahiti accounts for only a small percentage of the territory's production of copra (the dried white flesh of the coconut). Most of the commune's agricultural activity is concentrated in the coastal areas of Mataiea and Papeari. Dairy cattle are reared in Taravao, where citrus fruits—oranges in particular—and honey are also produced.

The greater part of French government spending in Tahiti goes to pay the high salaries of military personnel and public employees, such as these police officers.

The white flesh of the coconut is one of French Polynesia's major export products. Coconut oil and products also bring in significant income to the island of Tahiti.

BLACK PEARLS

The black pearl industry is the second-largest source of revenue for French Polynesia, after tourism. Black pearls are raised in more than 65 cooperatives and farms in the Tuamotu and Gambier Islands, where the *Pinctada margaritifera* (mother-of-pearl) oyster abounds.

To produce a pearl, a farmer introduces an implant (a tiny spherical object) into the oyster, which coats it with mother-of-pearl secretion. This process takes two years. Implantation is performed almost exclusively by Japanese specialists, although more Tahitians are becoming proficient at it. After implantation, the oysters are returned to the sea tied to long ropes. As many as 20,000 oysters are farmed at one time. But the success rate is very low: only 30–50 percent of the oysters actually produce a pearl.

Several types of pearls are harvested. *Keshis* are deformed pearls composed exclusively of mother-of-pearl. They occur when the implant is rejected by the oyster after it has been returned to the sea. Baroque pearls have imperfections in shape. Perfect pearls are smooth and round, with a metallic green-gray or blue-gray color. Only 3 percent of the harvest is perfect.

The cooperatives sell their pearls at an auction in Papeete every October. Local jewelers vie with Japanese buyers at these events, with more than 40,000 black pearls changing hands. Private farms sell their production through independent dealers or plush retail outlets in Papeete.

The east coast of Tahiti is devoted mostly to subsistence farming, but flowers (anthuriums, *opuhi*, and orchids) are grown on a large scale in the districts of Mahaena and Tiarei.

Despite the use of modern farming methods and machinery, agricultural production does not satisfy local demand. Many products are imported from other islands or other countries—Australia and New Zealand in particular. To make the situation worse, much of the land under cultivation is being taken over by residential development, especially in Papara, Mahaena, and Tiarei.

TRADE

Tahiti suffers from a severe imbalance in trade, with exports equaling only 20 percent of its imports. Nearly half of all imports come from France, which has imposed a series of self-favoring restrictions. Imports include food,

French Polynesia is a major producer of vanilla. This variety is native to the Pacific region and is called Vanilla tahitensis, *or Tahiti vanilla.*

The local lime is used in the preparation of raw fish and traditional medicine in Tahiti. Citrus fruits, coconuts, vanilla, and the *noni* plant are some of Tahiti's principal cash crops.

fuel, building materials, consumer goods, and automobiles. The main exports are copra, which is crushed into coconut oil and animal feed in a mill in Papeete, and cultured pearls. Copra and pearls are not produced on the island of Tahiti itself but in the Tuamotus and other outer islands. Exports of fish have steadily risen in the past few years, and this sector has been identified by the government as an important area of growth. Tahiti's main trading partners, apart from France, are the United States, Japan, Australia, New Zealand, and other islands in the Pacific.

TOURISM

Tourism started in earnest with the opening of the Faaa airport in 1961. Today it is the main revenue sector of French Polynesia's economy. From 1995 to 2004 receipts from tourism increased by more than 27 percent while capacity saw a 50 percent increase. One of the fastest-growing businesses in the tourist industry is the cruise sector.

One-third of all tourists come from the United States. Australian, Asian, and U.S. tourists regard Tahiti as a stopover destination, spending a couple of days in Papeete on their way to and from the United States. Tourists from France and other European countries stay longer but not always in hotels. Most of them come to visit relatives or friends who are expatriate workers in Tahiti.

Tourism in French Polynesia is still less developed than in Hawaii. High prices and the perceived distance from the United States, Europe, and Asia have kept tourist arrivals low. However, the French Polynesian authorities are targeting to achieve 300,000 tourist arrivals per year in

Bananas in Tahiti can be eaten cooked, raw, or both, depending on the species that is harvested. The multi-purpose plant is well-used in Tahiti. Its trunk is used for the construction of canoes, its sap serves as fuel, and its leaves make good tablecloths, plates, and food containers.

LAW OF THE SEA

When President Harry Truman declared U.S. sovereignty over the natural resources of an adjacent continental shelf in 1945, other countries followed suit, and in 1958 the United Nations convened the Conference on the Law of the Sea, which accepted national control over shelves up to 600 feet (183 m) deep. However, national claims multiplied so much that a second conference was convened, leading to the signing of the Law of the Sea in Jamaica in 1982.

The Law of the Sea states that a country can claim 12 nautical miles of sea off its shores as its territorial waters. (One international nautical mile is equal to around 1.15 miles or 1.85 km.) A country's continental shelf extends 200 nautical miles offshore. This area is called the Exclusive Economic Zone (EEZ), and the state has full control over all resources, living and nonliving, contained in the zone.

French Polynesia can lay claim to more than 3 million square miles (7.8 million square km) of the continental shelf, with immense possibilities for development. The National Marine Research Center estimates that vast mineral deposits, such as nickel, cobalt, manganese, and copper, are scattered across Tahiti's EEZ. While giving more political weight (and mineral wealth) to oceanic states, the Law of the Sea has also made French Polynesia much more valuable to France. The French government has adamantly refused to give the Territorial Assembly any jurisdiction over Tahiti's EEZ, a clear indication that it does not plan to let go of its sovereignty over the islands.

the next few years, a figure that is feasible according to experts from the French government. The most popular destinations for tourists are Tahiti, Moorea, Huahine, Raiatea, and Bora Bora.

FISHING

Although industrial fishing has long been dominated by Japanese, Korean, and U.S. purse seiners and long-line vessels, French Polynesia now has a professional fleet of 64 vessels trawling its territorial waters. As the government has targeted the fishing industry as a major source of future revenues, it has invested heavily in storage and packaging facilities as well. Much emphasis is placed on the training of fishermen (only men work on the fishing vessels) so that the industry is run in a more efficient and safe way. The catch is made up of deep-sea fish, mainly tuna, which is highly prized by the Japanese, as well as marlin and shark.

Most Tahitians fishing in the open sea still do so in *bonitiers* (boh-nee-TIAY), 36-foot (11-m) boats propelled by a powerful motor. A *bonitier* can take two or three fishers out for one day to about 30 miles (48 km) from shore. Fishing is done with lines, and the shoals of fish are detected by the presence of birds hovering above the sea. In addition, several sunken barges placed near the coast attract big fish and make it easier to locate large concentrations of fish.

Lagoon fishing is much more common throughout the islands. It is practiced in small wooden boats powered by outboard motors. Swift and light, they are ideal for catching flying fish or mahimahi (also known as

Fishing is practiced on a small scale by ordinary Tahitians. It is common to see fish strung out by the side of the road.

dorado or dolphin fish) that are harpooned as they swim by. Lagoon fishers are not professionals; most of them fish for their family meal. When they catch more fish than required, they keep it for the next day's meal.

LE TRUCK

Public transportation in Tahiti is provided by a network of privately owned minibuses called *le truck* (luh TRUCK). The driver's cabin is separated from the passengers' section by a panel, and the passenger door is at the back. Passengers sit on long wooden benches, and bags and other bulky items are piled on the roof of the vehicle. A notice advises passengers to hang their fish from the back of the minibus. The vehicles are painted in bright colors, and the network covers the whole island. The central terminal is near Papeete market, and the last trucks leave for the outlying districts at about 5 P.M. Around town, the service does not stop until 10 or 11 P.M. On Sundays, however, *le truck* does not run after noon.

The starting point—usually Papeete—and the final destination are indicated at the front of the vehicle. Other district names along the route are painted on the sides. No truck goes around the whole island, and long journeys involve catching several minibuses. In town and also in the districts of Pirae and Faaa, bus stops are designated by diagonal white lines painted on the street and sometimes with a sign. Elsewhere there is no specific bus stop; passengers just wave *le truck* down wherever they happen to be. There is no fixed schedule, but the vehicles are more frequent in and around Papeete. Fares are quite cheap and are usually posted on the side.

Inside the minibuses are mammoth speakers that often blast rock music or reggae. At night they take on a different look. Many have softly colored lights inside and play Tahitian ballads instead of loud music.

ENVIRONMENT

AN ENVIRONMENTAL STUDY CARRIED OUT in 1995 by an expert from respected conservation organization WWF (formerly the World Wildlife Fund) France noted the following major problems in French Polynesia: the poor quality of drinking water and the poor treatment of sewage; coral extraction for building purposes; and the spread of introduced plant species. Ten years later, the same expert came back to French Polynesia to conduct another study. While noting some improvements in the previously cited areas, she identified new areas of concern such as the evolution of biodiversity, air and water pollution, and noise control.

Because Tahiti depends so heavily on its "sun, sand, and sea" tourism, protection of its marine environment is of utmost importance and concern. Most hotels have sewage-treatment facilities and programs for recycling and protection of the beaches. Sustainable development and respect for the environment are regular themes during the annual youth festival organized by the Union pour la Jeunesse de Polynésie (Union of Polynesian Youths). In spite of industrial development, many areas of French Polynesia, even on heavily frequented islands such as Tahiti and Moorea, are still in pristine condition.

FORESTS

About 70 percent of Tahiti is covered with forest, mainly in Tahiti Nui and the mountainous interior of Tahiti Iti. However, Tahitian forests are not in a healthy state. Apart from encroachments by industrial developments and the human population, the native forest cover has been attacked by imported plant and animal species. Moreover, destructive hurricanes regularly top off the trees or stunt their growth.

A reforestation program has been in place since the late 1970s to replace the trees that are cut down for industrial usage. New seedlings

Opposite: **A view of the curtain of green vegetation over the imposing mountains of central Tahiti. As with many regions in the world today, the verdant forests of Tahiti and the biodiversity they sustain are also not spared from the threats of deforestation and the encroachment of urban development.**

comprise mainly the Caribbean pine, but mahogany and teak have also been planted on some islands. Although the program is supervised by the Ministry of Agriculture, the entire process of exploitation and replanting remains in the hands of the private sector.

One danger threatening Polynesian forests is the spread of introduced species such as the velvet tree, or miconia. French Polynesian authorities have experienced some measure of success with the release of a fungus that preys on miconia seedlings. *Colletotrichum gloeosporioides* destroys the leaves of mature velvet trees, causing the trees to die, and also kills the seedlings, especially germinating ones. This two-pronged attack deals with the problem literally at its root, by preventing the miconia seeds from growing into plants, and also by ensuring that mature plants do not reproduce.

In the 1990s the Tahitian sandalwood became endangered because its seeds were being eaten by rats. Following a rescue program, thousands of seeds were collected and planted in controlled areas. The success of the first planting has prompted the Polynesian authorities to enlarge the program to cover more islands.

MARINE ENVIRONMENT

Although 20 percent of the reefs around the urban areas have been destroyed, the coral population in the waters around Tahiti is one of the most stable in the world. In 2005 a team of 28 scientists from nine nations collected a large amount of coral samples that were dissected and studied to reveal changes in sea levels from as far back as 23,000 years ago. Most of the samples came from a location off Maraa, a point separating Tahiti's south and west coasts. The longest sample was 10 feet (3 m) long, representing 350 years of coral growth. Providing a

reliable climate record with no gaps, the corals helped the researchers to predict climate variability and piece together the frequency and amplitude of climatic anomalies such as El Niño. Because corals are ultrasensitive to environmental change, they provide a full record of temperature and salinity changes in the South Pacific over their lifetime.

Polynesian waters teem with fish. The most colorful are those living in the coral reefs. They also provide the main source of protein for the island population. Around 700 species of fish live in the lagoon or on the reef itself, feeding on the plentiful corals. Among the most attractive are the angelfish, the clown fish, and the damsel fish that live among the pink anemones. The larger parrot fish counts 25 varieties in French Polynesia. This brightly colored fish is often eaten raw in salads by the Tahitians. Jacks are also widely represented with 17 species, and there are a few varieties of mainly harmless lagoon shark. The latter are usually small and can swim in shallow water to look for food.

A diver with a school of stunning double-saddle butterfly fish in a lagoon of Tahiti. Tahiti is blessed with a wealth of delicate marine life forms and pristine coastal beauty.

ALIEN INVASION

Native to the tropical forests of Central America, the velvet tree (*Miconia calvescens*) was introduced into Tahiti in 1937 when Harrison W. Smith planted it in his private garden in Papeari. In less than 70 years, the spread of the species has been so rampant that it is now called "the green cancer" by the Tahitians.

Starting out as a shrub, the velvet tree eventually grows into a tree that can reach 50 feet (15 m) in height. Adorned with large velvety leaves, it produces fragrant clusters of pinkish white flowers and sweet purple berries. Because each berry contains between 50 and 200 seeds and the tree can fruit two or three times a year, the trees have spread at a phenomenal pace.

Miconia calvescens is a threat to the indigenous species of Tahiti because it has become so overwhelmingly dominant that it has taken over about 70 percent of the island's natural forest. Several factors have enabled the tree to proliferate: a lack of natural enemies; the low stature of local trees, which has allowed the velvet tree to tower above them; and a slow reaction by the Tahitian authorities to curb its spread. Moreover, the six hurricanes that hit Tahiti between December 1982 and April 1983 suppressed the growth of the natural forest canopy by breaking the tops of trees and destroying emergent native trees. French Polynesian ecologists estimate that between one-fourth and one-half of all endemic species are now at risk of extinction.

In 1988 the Miconia Research Program was put in place by the Tahitian authorities, and there are now a number of initiatives to slow the growth of the velvet tree.

Beyond the reef, in the open sea, larger varieties of fish live in deeper waters. Tuna and bonito are the most common. The latter can survive at depths of 900 feet (274 m) and has become a symbol of the Tahitian diet. Barracuda, dorado, and red perch also live in the ocean depths. Six species of marlin can be found in Tahiti, but three have become quite rare: the sailfish, the striped marlin, and the black marlin. The most common is the blue marlin, which can weigh up to a ton. Among the species of deep-sea sharks that frequent Polynesian waters, the gray shark is the most common, followed by the hammerhead shark. The tiger shark stays in deep water during the day and comes out in the channels at night.

Fishing is an important industry in Tahiti, and it is strictly regulated so that the fish stocks have time to renew themselves. Thanks to Tahiti's insistence on sound ecological practices, its marine environment has been quite well preserved. Even the underground nuclear testing on Moruroa and Fangataufa did not affect the level of fish in Polynesian waters. In fact, a recent study has found an unusually large amount of fish around the two atolls.

French Polynesia has actively protected whales and other aquatic mammals by setting up a sanctuary in Polynesian waters in 2002. This sanctuary covers the breeding grounds of the 24 species of whales that visit French Polynesia regularly, mainly the solitary blue whale, the sperm whale, and especially the humpback, which can be observed by boat between September and November. Rules governing the use of sonar and the distance between a craft and an animal as well as the speed of boats are enforced.

EFFECTS OF NUCLEAR TESTING

French nuclear activity in the Pacific spanned a period of 30 years. France conducted 41 atmospheric tests between 1966 and 1974, 140 underground tests between 1975 and 1991, and eight more underground tests in 1996. Some of them had a magnitude of 200 kilotons—10 times more powerful than the bomb that leveled the Japanese town of Hiroshima during World War II.

Throughout the testing period, and even to this day, the French authorities have maintained that those tests were clean, with no major repercussions on the local population. Their surveys showed that radiation levels were within limits, and the French defense ministry has always claimed that the data collected from those tests are military secrets.

However, the findings of a committee of inquiry set up by the French Polynesian assembly in 2006 painted a less rosy picture. Based on interviews with former CEP employees, studies of the incidence of cancer in French Polynesia, and 25 previously secret defense ministry documents, the committee found that the island of Tahiti itself was subjected to repeated fallout from each of the atmospheric tests more than 30 years ago. Radiation levels on Moruroa and Fangataufa were more than 100 times above the normal level even during the underground tests. Figures from the French Cancer Society show 600 cases of cancer and 250 related deaths a year in French Polynesia out of a total population of 250,000. One recent study indicated that 25.7 out of every 100,000 French Polynesian women contracted thyroid cancer, compared with 4.8 out of 100,000 in France. Leukemia, which typically manifests itself 15 to 20 years after radiation exposure, is also on the rise. Moreover, 7.4 percent of former Moruroa workers had physically disabled children, and 2.4 percent had mentally impaired offspring. Experts have also discovered that, even after more than 30 years, some people display chromosomal alterations stemming from irradiation or nuclear contamination.

Two groups of veterans from Moruroa and Fangataufa have set up associations to ask the French government to come clean on the effects of the tests. While the organization Moruroa e Tatou (Moruroa and Us) is quite strident and vocal, the newly formed Tamarii Moruroa (Children of Moruroa) highlights the positive effects of the tests (such as their application in the medical field) and has adopted a much more conciliatory tone. The former, in particular, is demanding compensation from the French government and has helped more than 200 former workers file class-action suits in the French courts.

In July 2006, 40 years after the first bomb was exploded in Moruroa, the French Polynesian government unveiled a memorial in Papeete to commemorate the 193 tests that had destabilized the region for 30 years. Built in the shape of a traditional *paepae* (PEA-pea), a log seat, with five stones symbolizing the five Polynesian archipelagoes, it is not a symbol of reconciliation with France but a sign of reconciliation among Polynesian peoples.

WASTE MANAGEMENT

Tahiti has embarked on an ambitious waste-management program that is unique in the Pacific. Aside from maintaining the infrastructure, the program provides the local population with in-depth education on recycling and waste disposal. The recycling center of Motu Uta receives more than 3,000 tons of waste a year, mainly glass, paper, drink cans, plastic bottles, and cardboard boxes, which are sorted and compacted before being exported overseas to be recycled in countries such as Singapore (50 percent), India (29 percent), and Australia (15 percent). However, recycling bins are available mainly on Tahiti and Moorea, and the next step for the Ministry of Environment is to reach out to the outer islands in terms of waste-management education.

Treatment of household and industrial waste is carried out at two plants in Tahiti: household and common industrial waste at Paihoro, and industrial and hazardous waste at the new incineration plant in Nivee.

Sewage treatment is carried out mainly in Tahiti, Moorea, and Bora Bora. The larger islands have been aware of the importance of water treatment for some years now, and the situation is quite positive. Although priority is given to those islands with a tourism infrastructure, the aim of the Polynesian authorities is to endow each sizable island with its own treatment plant. One of the themes for public environmental education is not to discard wastes into rivers, as these ultimately make their way to the sea and create an imbalance in the ecosystem.

The crystal-clear water surrounding the island is home to many marine species and sustains the economy of Tahiti.

TAHITIANS

ALL TAHITIANS are French citizens. Whatever their ethnic background, they enjoy the same constitutional rights as any other citizens of France.

More than 250,000 people live in French Polynesia, with nearly 70 percent living in Tahiti. Because large areas of Tahiti's land surface are not fit for human settlement, most of the island's inhabitants live in the coastal regions. About 65 percent of Tahitians live along the northwest coast, in and around Papeete, in the districts of Papeete, Pirae, Arue, and Mahina. This small area supports more than 3,000 people per square mile (1,875 per square km).

Tahiti and the island of Raiatea are the ethnic melting pots. The population on these islands is composed of Polynesians, Europeans (mainly French), Chinese, and people of mixed descent (Polynesian/ European, Polynesian/Chinese, and Chinese/European).

In Tahiti about 60 percent of the population is Polynesian, 15 percent European, 15 percent mixed, and 10 percent Chinese. Nearly half of the population is under the age of 20. People over the age of 60 account for only about 5 percent of the total population, the result of booming birth rates in the 1980s and 1990s.

Opposite: **A young native Tahitian boy.**

CHANGES IN TAHITI'S POPULATION

A graph of the population of Tahiti shows a sharp decline in the decades following the discovery of the island by the European explorers. However, since the beginning of the 20th century, the Tahitian population has been slowly rebuilding itself with lower infant-mortality rates and longer life expectancies and through immigration. Life expectancy in Tahiti has now risen to 72 years, compared with 79 years in France.

A tusk necklace and a headdress of palm fronds adorn this Polynesian man.

POLYNESIANS

The Polynesians were the first inhabitants of Tahiti. Their ancestors traveled by canoe from Southeast Asia to settle in the scattered islands of the Polynesian Triangle. They call themselves *Taata Maohi* (tah-AH-tah mah-OH-hee) or *Taata Tahiti,* meaning "people of Polynesia."

The Polynesian people have the same coloring as their distant ancestors: straight black hair, black eyes, and burnished skin. They have wide-set eyes, a round nose, and full lips. A sporty people, they tend to be well built and graceful. A sedentary modern lifestyle, however, is changing their physical profile, and obesity and its attendant health problems are becoming more pronounced.

Children are greatly cherished and valued in Polynesian society, and attractive government child benefits do not encourage family planning. For these reasons, Polynesian families tend to be large with as many as 10 children per family. In addition, adoption is a traditional feature of Polynesian society.

MAUI, THE POLYNESIAN SUPERHERO

Maui was a demigod who reveled in playing tricks and upsetting the status quo. One of his best-known exploits was slowing the passage of the sun. Before this feat, the sun used to race across the sky, and days were not long enough for people to beat out and dry tree bark for cloth, to grow and prepare food, and to build temples to the gods.

To slow down the sun, Maui braided several lassos, which he threw around the rays of the sun. They all broke, except the one made from the hair of his sister Hina. From then on the sun was bound to a boulder on the beach and traveled at a more convenient pace. As proof of this exploit, Tahitians point to his footprints, which can still be seen on the reef at Vairao on the peninsula.

Other feats performed by this superhero were lifting the sky high enough to permit people to walk upright, stealing fire from the gods and giving it to humans (making him the Polynesian equivalent of the mythical Greek hero Prometheus), and fishing all the islands of Polynesia out of the sea with a magical hook made from the jawbone of his grandmother. Maui was the archetypal hero who could deal with both gods and humans.

Like most other colonized peoples, the *Taata Maohi* have lost much of their land to the colonizers and are relegated to the bottom of the economic and social ladder. Most islanders outside of Tahiti are farmers, fishers, or manual workers. The Polynesian culture teaches a sense of sharing and reciprocal generosity, and the pursuit of money and material wealth is still, for the most part, alien. Unemployment is rife among Polynesians. Their economic and cultural situation has resulted in rising dissatisfaction with the French government and growing separatist, nationalistic feelings.

DEMIS

The offspring of early marriages between Polynesians and European colonizers, Demis (doh-MEE) are also called *Afa* (AH-fah) *Tahiti*, meaning "half Polynesian." The Demi population displays the whole spectrum of skin color typical of their ancestors, with many looking no different from Polynesians.

When the term *Demi* first appeared, it was used to designate those who started out as traders and landowners. Today, while there are many poor farmers among the Demis, this group is on the whole wealthier than the Polynesians. Indeed, *Demi* has come to signify those Polynesians or mixed-ancestry Polynesians who occupy high-status or powerful social positions or maintain a "European" lifestyle. Fluent in both French and Tahitian, the Demi population acts as a link between the French administration and the local people, although they identify more with European culture.

Contemporary Demis are now teachers, civil servants, and professionals. The largest business firms in the country are in the hands of a few Demi families. Generally speaking, these wealthy Demis do not identify at all with the Polynesians, although they have Polynesian relatives.

Historically prominent Demi families owned large tracts of land in Tahiti. When their European ancestors arrived in Tahiti, they married the daughters of the tribal chiefs. The land, which used to be owned collectively by the tribe, became the property of the chiefs at the time of colonization and was passed on from them to their mixed descendants. This was how the Salmon family, who come from the line of Queen Marau, the last queen of Tahiti, became one of the most prominent families in the country.

A Tahitian of Chinese descent.

CHINESE

The first Chinese came to Tahiti during the American Civil War, when the supply of cotton to Europe was disrupted. Later, in 1865 and 1866, a British colonizer recruited 1,010 laborers from the southern Chinese province of Guangdong to work in the cotton fields of Atimaono because the local Polynesians could not be persuaded to do such heavy work. However, at the end of the war the cotton industry went bankrupt, and most of these workers returned to China.

About 300 Chinese stayed on in Tahiti, taking gardening jobs or becoming shopkeepers. They were joined in 1910 by a group of immigrants fleeing the poverty of their native land. Chinese immigration did not end until World War II. As the government did little to integrate the *Tinito* (tee-NEE-toh), or Chinese, community into Tahitian society, refusing to grant them the right to own land and barring them from many professions, the Chinese immigrants turned their energy to the retail trade. Within a few decades they were in control of the retail trade and of transactions involving vanilla, as well as mother-of-pearl, and were making large capital investments in maritime transportation too.

Young Polynesian children.

In 1964 the French government decided to assimilate the Chinese community by granting them citizenship, requiring that they adopt French names, and closing all Chinese schools. Despite becoming French citizens, the Chinese community is still distinct through the maintenance of language and ancestral customs by way of cultural associations and clan groups. The Chinese shopkeeper is a common sight in all the islands of French Polynesia, and entire streets in Papeete are lined with Chinese stores.

POPAA

All white people are called *Popaa* (poh-pah-AH), meaning "foreigner," by the Tahitians. The French are also called *Popaa Farani* (poh-pah-AH fah-rah-NEE). There is no traditional white community in Tahiti, because

Tahitian women in traditional Tahitian regalia—brightly printed dresses and wreaths of flowers on their heads.

the former colonizers married Polynesian women, and their descendants are Demis rather than Popaa. Most Popaa are French soldiers and civil servants and are only temporary residents in Tahiti. After the closure of the CEP, the French population decreased by half, with around 10,000 left. There had been considerable European immigration in the 1960s and 1970s associated with the setting up of the CEP.

Now that the military presence in Tahiti is greatly reduced due to the closure of the CEP, there is a better statistical balance between the sexes among the Popaa, with only slightly more males than females. On the whole, the Popaa community is young and open to change.

Many Popaa come to Tahiti, live and work in the country, but leave without ever truly assimilating into Polynesian society. Because of the high salaries and other perks offered to French civil servants and administrators, a tour of duty in Tahiti is highly desirable and is treated like a long vacation.

TAHITIAN DRESS

The image that has gone around the world of the bare-breasted *vahine* (vah-HEE-nay), or woman, dressed in a grass skirt with a garland of flowers around her neck can be found only on tourist brochures. The traditional dress for both men and women is the pareu, a 6-foot (1.8-m) length of cotton cloth printed with bright designs, usually flowers. There are several ways for women to

Tahitian women in traditional clothes.

wear a pareu. The simplest is to wrap the cloth around the body and tuck the ends in. For a more secure fit, the pareu is wrapped around the body, with one corner thrown over the right shoulder, the other corner passed under the left arm, and the two ends tied at the neck. Men wear the pareu as a loincloth, tied around the waist.

When the missionaries arrived in Tahiti, they were shocked by the state of undress of the women in particular and designed a "mission dress" for them. This is a loose cotton dress with wrist- or elbow-length sleeves, much like a nightgown. Cool and comfortable, it is still worn by Tahitian women and is the uniform of *himene* (hee-MAY-nay), or singing, groups.

Most Tahitians, however, dress in stylish Western clothes. Young girls wear jeans and T-shirts or skirts and blouses. At the beach or for casual wear, shorts and cropped tops are common. Tahitian men wear shirts and trousers to work and are often dressed in shorts and T-shirts at home. Men and women put on shoes to go out, although it is customary to remove their shoes in the house.

LIFESTYLE

MOST OF THE POPULATION of Tahiti is concentrated in and around Papeete. Residents work in the airport, at the docks, and in businesses in town. The rural Tahitians are farmers and fishers, mostly at subsistence level.

Great differences in income have created several distinct social classes, and because the cost of living is very high, many Tahitians live on the brink of poverty. In addition, high unemployment among the young has resulted in severe social problems such as drug addiction, alcoholism, and crime.

However, in spite of difficult living conditions, the Tahitian people have not lost their ability to enjoy themselves. They take pleasure in simple activities, such as listening to music or riding around the island on their scooters.

CLASS STRUCTURE

The Tahitian social structure is very much related to the ethnic backgrounds of the people. The Popaa are at the top of the social ladder, followed by the Demis and the Chinese, with the Polynesians at the bottom. Even so, class stratification is based not so much on heritage as on affluence.

UPPER CLASS The upper class is formed by the French civil servants and administrators, who are paid salaries that are almost double those of their counterparts in France. However, while they receive generous expatriation benefits, they also incur high expenses if they want to consume French products, since these tend to be very expensive. Most Popaa government officials serve a three- or four-year term in the territory, at the end of which they are entitled to six months' paid leave. Although they try to get into the spirit of life in Polynesia, by wearing flowery shirts to

Opposite: **A Tahitian family smiles for the camera. Tahitians enjoy the wealth of vegetation and natural coastal beauty Tahiti has to offer.**

work, for example, the ruling class lives apart from the local population. The French officials' exalted status attracts much resentment from the local population, who would like to see fewer of them and more of their own people in charge of their country.

MIDDLE CLASS   The middle class is made up of Demis—people of mixed ancestry. Although some Demis are far more affluent than the Popaa, they are not considered to be on an equal footing with the French community. Many Demis families are wealthy landowners who derive their income from leasing the land to farmers or developing their property into commercial ventures. Because they have always had access to formal education, the Demis often hold jobs in the government service and in professional occupations and still keep a strong hold on the business sector. They are generally fluent in French, and many can also speak English. Culturally closer to their European roots, they are faced with a situation where the two sides of their ancestry are at odds with each other. Economically powerful, they do not have any political clout. However, most Demis are against independence and side with the French population on political matters.

In terms of income, the Chinese community also belongs to the middle class. Having succeeded in the retail trade, the Chinese have moved into bigger businesses and bought up large areas of property since being granted French citizenship. Today most Chinese manage their own businesses, and many of the young people, having received a formal French education, are professionals. They are not formally represented in the government as a group, but some politicians are of mixed Chinese ancestry. The Chinese have economic power, but they have no cultural ties with the traditional *Demi* middle class. Having long been viewed as an economic threat to the local upper class, this community has been slowly assimilating into Tahitian society through marriage with Polynesians and Popaa, forming a new, ethnically different Demi group. The Chinese community is politically fragmented, with one group favoring independence and the other preferring the status quo that has allowed them to amass their wealth.

LOWER CLASS The lower class is formed primarily of the majority Polynesian ethnic group. Despoiled of their land during colonization, most rural Polynesians subsist on farms rented from the wealthy landowners. Those who own land are vegetable farmers, supplementing their diet with fish that they catch themselves. Most other Polynesians are employed as manual workers, in the construction industry, or in tourism. Unemployment among Polynesians is very high. The outskirts of the capital are surrounded by slums where crime and prostitution are rife. In the shantytowns behind Papeete and Faaa, there are typically 10 to 15 Polynesians living crammed into each neat flower-decked plywood house. Polynesian families tend to be larger than those of other ethnic groups. Disaffected Polynesian youths were responsible for much of the looting and violence committed during the antinuclear protests of September 1995. The poor urban communities view independence from France as their only means of salvation.

A small group of poor Demis is also part of the lower class. Because of their poverty, they feel closer to the Polynesian section of the population. For all intents and purposes, these Demis are treated as Polynesians.

THE TAHITIAN HOUSE

The traditional Tahitian residence consists of several separate buildings instead of rooms. The *fare tutu* (fah-RAY too-TOO) is the kitchen, while the dining area is the *fare tamaa* (fah-RAY tah-MAH-ah). The

A modern version of the traditional Tahitian house, made of painted plywood and thatched with palm leaves.

sleeping quarters are located in another building called the *fare taoto* (fah-RAY tah-OH-toh). In addition, toilet and bathing facilities are located in separate buildings. The traditional building materials are coconut trunks and pandanus leaves.

Today very few Tahitians live in traditional houses. Traditional design has been replaced by Western architectural models. In the rural areas, houses are square, built of wood, and covered with a sloping thatch roof. In the affluent suburbs of Papeete, people live in beautiful detached houses made of concrete and fronted by flower-filled gardens. Most working-class Tahitians, however, live in double-story row houses made of plywood. These are small, afford almost no privacy, and have no garden. Although such houses are ugly and uncomfortable, public housing is still better than the slums, where several families share a house and as many as 20 people live in one room.

HEALTH CARE

Health care in Tahiti is of the same standard as that in France, with doctors in Papeete's Mamao Hospital treating almost every type of disease and the former military hospital of Jean Prince in Pirae specializing in cardiology. The hospitals in the other towns all possess an operating room, but severe cases are sent to Papeete.

Tahitians have three health-care options: traditional remedies, private doctors, and public health services. *Raau* (rah-AH-oo) *Tahiti*, or traditional medicine, is composed of herbal remedies prepared at home, which

> **RAAU TAHITI**
>
> Some traditional medical treatments do not involve the preparation of herbal remedies. For instance, if you are stung by a sea urchin, just urinate on the injury. If stung by the crown-of-thorns starfish, turn the animal over and apply it to the wound; the suckers on the stomach of the starfish suck out the spines and venom. The stings of the scorpion fish and the stonefish are treated by bathing the wound with the water contained in small black sea cucumbers.

are quite effective in the treatment of pains and aches, coughs, and fever. Traditional remedies are still very popular for cultural reasons and also because they are cheap. The traditional medicine man is called a *tahua* (tah-HOO-ah) and gives treatments for free. Most people do not actually consult a *tahua*, because the recipes for common remedies are passed down in the family from one generation to the next.

Private medical facilities are good but more costly in comparison with public health services. They include general practitioners, specialists, and dentists. Two modern clinics—Paofai and Cardella—in Papeete offer surgical and maternity facilities. They also employ a number of doctors who give consultations to the sick. Public health care is free and available at dispensaries, polyclinics, and hospitals. Schoolchildren receive regular free health screenings.

EDUCATION

Tahitian children follow the French system of education. Schooling is compulsory between the ages of 5 and 16. After secondary school, the better students study three more years for the baccalaureate exams. Those who pass receive nearly free university education.

The French Polynesian government is in charge of primary and secondary education, while tertiary education is still the domain of the French government. Tahitian children study a hybrid curriculum, learning both French and Tahitian language and literature and the history and geography of both France and their own part of the world. The best students are given scholarships by the government to further their studies. Those who are not academically inclined move on to vocational training in a Centre de Jeunes Adolescents (CJA). They start at the age of 13 and stay for four years.

There are two types of schools: government schools, which are free, and fee-paying private schools, usually run by the churches. Most primary schools are public, but more than half of the young people of Papeete attend a private secondary school. Many of the private schools receive government funding. In exchange for this, they must follow the same curriculum as government schools.

Tertiary education is provided by the Université de la Polynésie Française in Faaa. Started in 1987 as the Polynesian branch of the Université Française du Pacifique, it has about 2,000 students and 60 researchers studying law, the physical sciences, and the humanities.

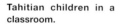

Tahitian children in a classroom.

ALCOHOLISM AND DRUG ABUSE

One of the scourges of Tahiti, alcoholism is a source of major social dysfunction in Tahitian society, particularly among Polynesians and other lower-income groups. Drinking beer is almost a rite of passage for young boys, who see it as taking a step into the adult world. The usual age at which boys start drinking alcohol is around 14. Drinking is very common among the lower class, and alcoholism and its negative effects are seen as unavoidable. Indeed, Tahitians are often impressed by good drinkers, and the ability to consume large amounts of alcohol can even be a source of pride. Excessive drinking is a problem that also affects women and girls. Domestic violence is the most frequent consequence of excessive consumption of alcohol. Another consequence is road accidents caused by drunk driving.

Drug addiction is not as prevalent as drunkenness but is cause for concern, with children as young as 10 years old having been caught abusing solvents. Hard drugs, such as heroin and cocaine, are still relatively uncommon in Tahiti, but the cultivation of marijuana by small-scale traffickers is spreading in the humid, mountainous regions of the interior.

SOCIAL PROBLEMS

One of the main problems faced by Tahitian society today is unemployment. The unemployed consist mainly of women, young people, people with few skills, and Polynesians. More than half of the people looking for work are in the 18–24 age group. They are the product of an educational system that does not take into consideration local needs. Many of those who do have a certificate are not qualified for the types of jobs that are available. In addition to the unemployed, there are wage earners who are employed on a periodic basis. Frequently out of work but not registered as unemployed, they account for as much as 30 percent of the labor force.

Resulting directly from the problem of unemployment is that of delinquency. This problem affects mostly young Polynesians who have dropped out of school at 16—the age when compulsory education ends—and are waiting to enlist in the military. With a lot of time on their hands and little money, and tempted by Papeete's consumer society, they turn to petty crime such as theft. Young delinquents from low-income families live outside social norms. They tend to live in groups and call themselves *hombos* (HOM-boh). The word derives from the Spanish

"We debauch their morals and introduce among them wants and diseases which they never before knew, and which disturb the happy tranquility which they enjoyed."

—*Captain James Cook*

Unemployment is a major problem. Polynesians who come from other islands and are unable to find work may end up living on the street or in a slum.

hombre (man) and is used to describe "antiheroes" such as Mexican and U.S. outlaws and comic-book characters.

Many sociologists see the rise in delinquency as having social and cultural, rather than economic, roots. They believe that these young Polynesians turn to petty crime because they are confused about their own cultural identity, living in a world with two different, often conflicting, cultures—Polynesian and French.

VAHINE

Two centuries ago Bougainville wrote that Tahitian *vahine* were as pretty as European women and better proportioned. Since then, the myth of the gentle women of Tahiti, half-naked and beckoning to all new male arrivals, has taken root in Western imagination. The romanticized *vahine* has long black hair, a slim and supple body, and a bewitching smile.

Most Tahitian women are indeed pretty, graceful, and stylish. Women of all ages like to wear colorful hibiscus or frangipani blooms in their hair and clothes of bright, vivid colors. Even the simplest housedress is

THE THIRD SEX

Polynesia's *mahus* (mah-HOO) suffer little of the stigma attached to transvestites in the West. When the missionaries first arrived in Tahiti, they were shocked to discover that not only did the *mahus* exist but also that they were encouraged to take on the jobs women normally did. They looked after children, worked as maids, and cooked, all the while wearing women's clothes or whatever else they wanted to wear. In festival performances and celebrations, they sometimes assumed the roles played by women.

A young boy may adopt the female role in society by his own choice or by that of his parents, performing domestic tasks designated for women and eventually finding a job usually performed by women, such as waiting on tables in a restaurant, cleaning rooms in a hotel, or working as a bartender. Usually only one *mahu* exists in each village or community, evidence that the *mahu* serves a certain sociological function in Tahitian society.

Though Tahitians may poke fun at *mahus*, they are fully accepted in society, with some even teaching Sunday school. Many, but not all, *mahus* are homosexual. Today some clubs in Papeete feature striptease acts by *mahus*, and some transvestites also engage in prostitution. The term *raerae* has been coined to describe male prostitutes. *Mahus* even have special beauty contests, such as Miss Raerae or Miss Tane (*tane* is Tahitian for "man").

worn with style. Tahitian women wear very little jewelry, preferring the flowers that grow in profusion on their island. The art of making flower garlands and headdresses is passed down from mother to daughter. The flowers are picked before sunrise, and it takes approximately a half-hour to make one simple headdress.

In the days when the first European explorers marveled at their apparent freedom, Tahitian women were in fact treated as second-class citizens. They were considered impure, and most families did not value their daughters highly. Modern Tahitian society is plagued by high incidences of rape. Sexual violence is the second most common crime in Tahiti, and Polynesian society still punishes it with a certain ambivalence. In general, however, Tahitian men show a respectful attitude toward women. Male–female greetings in public are usually limited to a smile and a "hello" or a wave.

Today's *vahine* enjoy more equality with men. Tahitian women are given the same educational opportunities as men, and they work as teachers, scientists, and truck drivers.

RELIGION

ALTHOUGH TAHITI IS A TERRITORY of France, a country where the main religion is Roman Catholicism, the majority of Tahitians are Protestants of the Evangelical Church. This is because the first Europeans to settle on the island were Protestant missionaries from the London Missionary Society. After an unsuccessful early attempt, Catholic missionaries returned 39 years after the Protestant missionaries, and the Mormons followed eight years later. Today, in addition to the Evangelical, Catholic, and Mormon churches, Seventh-Day Adventists, Jehovah's Witnesses, and Sanitos are represented in Tahiti. A few among the Chinese populace are Buddhists.

The population of Tahiti is deeply religious, despite decades of secular living. Church attendance is very high, and many children attend schools run by the churches. In the outer islands, priests and local ministers wield considerable influence. Although the government recognizes no official religion, members of the Territorial Assembly say a few collective prayers before the start of the session.

Prior to the introduction of Christianity at the end of the 18th century, Tahitians had their own ancient religion. They believed in the immortality of the soul, in a heavenly paradise, and in reincarnation as another creature "on land, in the sea, or in the skies." When King Pomare II became a Christian, many sacred statues and other religious symbols were destroyed. The conversion to Christianity was total, and there are no followers of the ancient religion today.

Above and opposite: **In Tahiti, attending church is a communal affair.**

THE EVANGELICAL CHURCH

More than half of the population of Tahiti is Protestant. The first missionaries from the London Missionary Society arrived in 1797. Made up of Presbyterians, Methodists, and Episcopalians, the mission did not meet with success until 1812, when King Pomare II converted to the new faith for strategic reasons. Thereafter all Tahitians became Christians, and the Pomare rulers staunchly upheld their faith. So influential were the Evangelical missionaries that one of them, George Pritchard, tried to convince Queen Pomare IV to petition the English king to make Tahiti a British protectorate. This started a conflict with the French that led to the eventual annexation of Tahiti by France.

White dresses, white straw hats, and formal suits are typical attire worn by those attending a Tahitian church service.

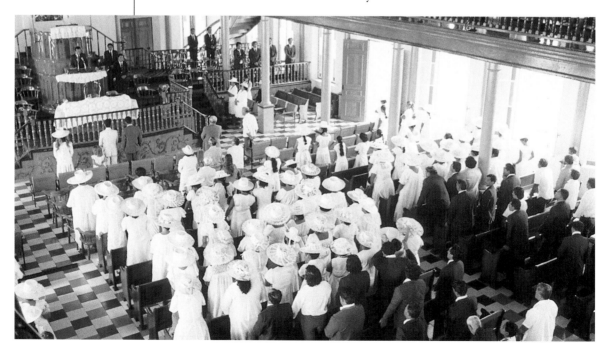

The Evangelical Church

The Tahitian population was initially very hostile to Christianity, yet there were many similarities between their traditional religion and the Christian faith: *Maohi* legends that resemble Biblical stories; the existence of a God, creator of the universe; and the belief in an immortal soul. After the initial wariness and reticence of Tahitians wore off, these similarities must have facilitated the implantation of Christianity in Tahiti. Also, Polynesian belief systems allowed for the possibility of adopting new and more powerful gods, such as those followed by conquering chiefs. Thus, the technological superiority displayed by the Europeans could have been interpreted as a sign of a more powerful god who was worthy of adoption.

Today the Evangelical Church in Tahiti is independent, looking solely to the Bible for guidance. The church is organized into 27 parishes, each

The Bible was translated into Tahitian by King Pomare II.

A CHURCH WITH A SOCIAL CONSCIENCE

The Evangelical Church in Tahiti actively promotes the improvement of the Tahitian people. In order to do so, it runs several schools that were models of education well before the first government school was built. Evangelical schools offer a secular education, in line with the government's policy, and are open to children of all faiths. Instead of teaching religious precepts, they place more emphasis on the personality of the students and their sense of responsibility.

The church shoulders its fair share of social responsibility through its youth movements and rehabilitation centers. Its leaders are very outspoken on social issues and have stated their opposition to nuclear testing on many occasions. They are always willing to meet with government officials to discuss problems facing Tahitian society, such as inflation, pollution, and alcoholism. The Evangelical Church takes its role as pastoral guide seriously.

led by a pastor and a council of deacons. Each parish consists of various pastoral groups headed by a deacon. Each group is entrusted with various tasks within the community. In addition to the church building, there is a parish house that acts as a meeting place for the congregation. Sunday school is conducted in this building. The most important church in Tahiti is that of Paofai in Papeete.

Sunday services are well attended, with most parishioners dressed smartly in white. Most women wear a modernized version of the mission dress and a white hat. Services are conducted in Tahitian and last up to two hours. The whole congregation joins the choir in singing beautiful hymns or songs of worship and praise.

THE CATHOLIC CHURCH

The first attempt at converting the Tahitians to Catholicism took place in 1774, when two Franciscan priests were left on the island to spread the faith. They were so fainthearted that the mission failed dismally. Mistaking the curiosity of the natives for aggression, the priests locked themselves up in the mission building and concluded that Tahiti was too dangerous for them. They went back to Peru one year later, leaving no trace of their passage.

The next Catholic missionaries arrived from France in 1834 but were sent away by Queen Pomare IV upon the advice of the British missionary and consul George Pritchard. It was not until the French established the protectorate that the Catholic Church gained more influence.

Today half of the people in northern Tahiti are Catholic—mainly the Popaa government workers. They are concentrated in the urban region between Paea and Mahina, where most French expatriates live. Overall 30 percent of the population of French Polynesia is Catholic.

Opposite: **A Catholic church in Taravao.**

The Catholic Church is very influential in the field of social services. It runs 17 primary schools and secondary schools in Tahiti. One of the largest is La Mennais, a Catholic middle and high school in Papeete with more than 2,000 students, and Anne-Marie Javouhey College in Papeete, which has about 1,000 students. The church is also active in the formation and running of youth organizations, including the Boy Scouts and the Sporting and Cultural Federation of France. In addition, the church conducts family-planning classes, organizes counseling sessions for families, and prepares young people for married life. The use of the media is vital for the church to reach as many Tahitians as possible. Two Catholic newspapers are published, a bimonthly in French and a monthly in Tahitian. The Tepano Jaussen Center also prepares radio and television programs.

There are 34 Catholic churches in Tahiti, most of them in the urban sprawl of Papeete. The oldest and most important is Notre Dame Cathedral, built in 1875. Many new church buildings reflect modern architectural trends. The Saint Etienne Church in Punaauia has an interesting facade of overlapping triangles. Services are usually conducted in French and are characterized by immense fervor and beautiful singing.

THE LONGEST TEMPLE IN THE WORLD

After King Pomare II became a Christian, he decided to emulate the biblical King Solomon and build a temple larger than that of Jerusalem.

Knowing nothing about Hebrew or European architecture, he based his temple on a traditional oval hut, using native timber and palm leaves. This method of construction enabled the temple to be built in less than a year. The central roof ridge rested on 36 pillars made of full-length breadfruit trees, and the lower edges of the roof rested on 280 shorter pillars of the same material. The walls, straight on the long sides but circular at the short ends, were made of sawed planks. The roof was covered with pandanus leaves.

Called the Royal Mission Chapel, the temple was 712 feet (217 m) long. However, due to the insufficiency of building materials and construction techniques, the width was only 54 feet (16.5 m) and the height 18 feet (5.5 m). By comparison, Saint Peter's Basilica in Rome is 616 feet (188 m) long, 379 feet (115.5 m) wide, and 151 feet (46 m) high (without the cupola). The Royal Mission Chapel had 29 doors and 133 windows with sliding shutters to let in air and light. Because of its strange proportions, it looked more like a huge, flattened cowshed than the awe-inspiring monument that its builder intended it to be.

The corridor-shaped building could accommodate a congregation of 6,000 people, as happened once or twice a year during the general church assemblies. However, no preacher could make himself heard by everyone. This problem was eventually solved by the erection of three pulpits: the first in the eastern nave, where the king sat with his nobles on wooden benches; the second in the middle; and the third in the western nave, where the commoners sat on a layer of dry grass spread out on the floor. The separation of the social classes was facilitated by a natural obstacle: a river 5 feet (1.5 m) wide, which the builders had not been able to divert, flowing diagonally across the floor.

With the death of Pomare II in 1821, the Royal Mission Chapel began to decay. It was eventually replaced by a wooden church of more manageable size, which was torn down at the end of the 19th century to make way for a charming 12-sided chapel. This was replaced by a slightly larger one in 1978.

Opposite: **The facade of the Mataiea Protestant Church in Tahiti.**

OTHER CHURCHES

Five smaller churches are active in Tahiti: the Church of Jesus Christ of Latter-day Saints (Mormons), the Reorganized Church of Jesus Christ of Latter-day Saints (Sanitos), Seventh-Day Adventists, Jehovah's Witnesses, and the Pentecostal Movement. Young Mormon missionaries continue to flock to Tahiti from the United States for two-year stays. They travel in pairs and are easily recognizable by their attire: short-sleeve white shirts with a tie. All five churches are characterized by the payment of tithes and their rejection of the established churches.

The Mormons, the Sanitos, and the Seventh-Day Adventists run their own schools and organize activities for young people and women. Emphasis is placed on the family, and training and personal development are considered important to improve oneself economically. The Jehovah's Witnesses and the Pentecostals do not have much of a social agenda. Growing dissatisfaction with the established churches coupled with the proselytizing efforts of the smaller churches ensure that these less-established religions will have a growing influence.

POLYNESIAN FAITH

The ancient Polynesian world was inhabited with gods, demigods, spirits, and elves, all of whom could move freely between this world and theirs. The gods were represented by carved figures called tikis. The spiritual power of the gods rested in the *mana*, the essence of divine authority with which high chiefs were also endowed.

The most important place of worship was the *marae* (mah-RAH-ay), a rectangular area covered with paving stones and surrounded by low walls. The altar, in the form of a step pyramid, stood at one end. Worshippers asked for the gods' blessings by making offerings of fruits, vegetables, fish, pigs, and dogs, which were placed on wooden platforms. Once the gods had sampled each food, the priests carrying out the ceremony consumed the rest.

Human sacrifices were carried out in times of great crisis. Only men could be sacrificed, as women were considered ill-suited vessels for the gods. The victim was ambushed and killed elsewhere before being offered to the gods.

Many restrictions called *tapu* (the origin of the English word "taboo") were observed. Although Tahitians have been Christians for almost 200 years, there are those who remain wary of going too close to the ancient places of worship.

The mythic themes of Polynesian religion helped to justify rank and social stratification to a people concerned with genealogy, respect and disrespect, and aspects of nature that needed to be explained and, if possible, appeased. The Polynesian religion was an outgrowth of the Polynesian social structure, which focused on genealogical connections and the integration of the gods with nature and the human condition.

THE CREATION OF THE WORLD

According to the ancient Tahitians, a great octopus held the sky and the earth together in its arms. The god Taaroa existed in the darkness of contemplation, and from this darkness he called the other gods into being. When Taaroa shook himself, feathers fell and turned into trees, plantains, and other green plants. Rua (the Abyss) killed the octopus by a magic trick, but that did not release his hold on the universe, and the demigods Ru, Hina, and Maui were born in the darkness. Ru raised the sky as high as the coral tree but ruptured himself, so his intestines floated away to become the clouds that usually hang over the island of Bora Bora. Maui, the trickster, then used wedges to support the sky and went to enlist the help of Tane, who lived in the highest heaven. Tane drilled into the sky with a shell until light came through. The arms of the octopus fell away and became the island of Tubuai. Tane then decorated the sky with stars and set the sun and moon on their courses. The fish and other sea creatures were given places and duties, and the god Tohu was assigned the job of painting the beautiful color on the fishes and the shells of the deep. In Tahiti, Tane is symbolized by a piece of finely braided coconut-fiber rope.

Opposite: **This young woman wears a gold cross around her neck with her traditional Polynesian dress. The ancient Polynesian religion has disappeared from Tahiti forever.**

85

LANGUAGE

TAHITI HAS TWO OFFICIAL LANGUAGES: Tahitian and French. Official documents and speeches are generally in French and are rarely translated. Most people are fluent in French, although some Polynesians, particularly those from the lower strata of Tahitian society, speak only Tahitian. Many of the expatriate civil servants, on the other hand, do not understand Tahitian.

English is taught as a third language in some secondary schools, and many educated Demis and Chinese can speak it quite well. Most people employed in the tourist industry can manage a simple conversation in English. Large Chinese stores also have someone who can speak English, although most Chinese use Hakka, a Chinese dialect, among themselves.

THE TAHITIAN LANGUAGE

Tahitian is one of a family of Austronesian languages spoken from Madagascar in the Indian Ocean through Indonesia all the way to Easter Island and Hawaii. Among Polynesian languages, those of Eastern Polynesia and New Zealand (Tahitian, Hawaiian, Maori) are quite different from those of Western Polynesia (Samoan, Tongan). Within French Polynesia, the Tahitian language is spoken mainly in the Society Islands. However, with the improvement of interisland communications and the growing dominance of Tahiti over the rest of the territory, the dialects in the outer islands are increasingly influenced by Tahitian.

Above: **A student studying a book on Tahitian grammar.**

Opposite: **French and English books in a bookstore in Tahiti.**

TAHITIAN PRONUNCIATION

Consonants

f	as in *four*
h	as in *home*, except when it is preceded by *i* and followed by *o* or *u*; then it sounds like *sh*
m	as in *man*
n	as in *nine*
p	as in *super*, while blowing as little air as possible
r	a rolled sound produced by caving in the tip of the tongue, similar to the French pronunciation
t	as in *paste*, with no explosion of air
v	as in *vain*, but sometimes also pronounced like a *w* or almost like a *b* with both lips touching

In some words, *r* and *n* are used interchangeably; *f* and *h* are also used as variants of each other.

Vowels

a	as in *ah*
e	as in *pay*
i	as in *till*
o	as in *hose*
u	as in *good*

Long vowels are read the same as listed above but pronounced as if they were doubled.

A traditional Tahitian phrase of welcome is "Ia orana!"

There are eight consonants in Tahitian (*f, h, m, n, p, r, t, v*) and five vowels (*a, e, i, o, u*). Vowels can be either long or short. The small number of letters means that many words are spelled the same way; the difference is indicated by how long the vowel is held when pronounced. One interesting feature of Tahitian words is the inclusion of two or three consecutive vowels, sometimes the same vowel (as in *Faaa*). Each vowel is pronounced separately, except for *ai, au, ae,* and *oi*, which are usually pronounced as diphthongs. There are no appearances of two consecutive consonants. An important sound in the Tahitian language is the glottal stop, which usually separates two vowel sounds. The glottal stop is produced by raising the back of the mouth to block the flow of air before pronouncing the next vowel. Two words spelled the same way can be differentiated by the use of the glottal stop. In written texts, it is sometimes represented by an apostrophe.

A sentence is made up of the verb, the subject, and the object, in this order. Nouns do not have singular and plural forms, nor do they have gender. To denote the plural, the word *mau* (mah-OO) is added before the noun. To denote the masculine, the word *tane* (tah-NAY), or "man," follows the noun, while the word *vahine*, or "woman," following the noun means that it is a feminine word.

Just like any other living language, Tahitian is constantly changing. The influence of English is evident in the following words: *faraipani* (frying pan), *moni* (money), *painapo* (pineapple), and *tapitana* (captain). These influences, however, are not recent but date back to initial contact with English missionaries in particular.

The Tahitian language had no written form until the first missionaries set about recording it. History, customs, and traditions were passed down from one generation to the next by word of mouth.

FRENCH

In Tahiti, French is not regarded as being more prestigious than Tahitian. Its usage depends greatly on the speaker's ability to gain access to education and the educational level attained. Demi families, having had access to education for several generations, are very fluent in both languages. They use French at home and on social occasions. Tahitian is spoken by "Polynesian" families (regardless of ethnicity), who have maintained the language in spite of restrictions on its usage in the school systems prior to the 1980s. However, proper French is less widely used by poor Demi families in rural areas, where access to education may be limited.

Tahiti has a minor export industry in the production of postage stamps. Although the quality of the graphics and production has tended to be uneven, the stamps are now in demand among overseas collectors. Stamps also serve as advertising for Tahiti.

This colorful sign, written in French and Tahitian, promotes an antilitter campaign.

French is the working language in Papeete. In general, all official matters are conducted in it. And of course, school is taught in French. The Tahitians speak French with a flourish, giving it a special richness with their rolled *r's*.

NEWSPAPERS

The press in Tahiti has a very short history. Officially there was a state-run newspaper in existence called *Messager de Tahiti* (1852–82). But the first modern newspaper, *Les Nouvelles de Tahiti,* only hit the newsstands in 1957. Today the daily readership of 30,000 is split between *Nouvelles* and *La Dépêche de Tahiti*, which was first published in 1964. Both papers are in French and come out in the morning. *La Dépêche* is larger, with more international news. In 1989 the locally owned *Nouvelles* was purchased by French publishing magnate Robert Hersant, who also owns *La Dépêche*.

Both dailies publish news of general interest, including politics, current affairs, sports, and entertainment. Coverage of local news and events is quite comprehensive, although the newspapers are now devoting more space to the outer islands and the Pacific region as a whole.

Reporting is usually free and independent, but both papers tend to be pro-French. There is a free weekly newspaper that is published in English. It is targeted at the tourist market and covers only news that is relevant to tourists. There is also an English magazine, the monthly *Tahiti Sun Press*. There is no national newspaper in Tahitian.

Tahitipresse, a daily electronic newspaper, is accessed by more than 30,000 readers on a regular basis. Although it receives financial support from the government, its coverage of local and regional news is widely regarded as fair and unbiased. Only one-third of its readers reside in Tahiti. The rest are mainly Tahitians living overseas or former expatriates who have worked and resided in Tahiti.

RADIO AND TELEVISION

Radio operations started in 1935 with a small group of amateur wireless operators broadcasting news and entertainment after 6 P.M. every day. The first radio station, Radio Tahiti—La Voix de France, was established in 1949, with programs in French and Tahitian. It has now been absorbed by the state-controlled RFO (Radio France d'Outre-Mer), which also broadcasts in the other French overseas departments and territories. The aim of RFO is to educate and reach out to as many listeners as possible. Its programs cater to every socioeconomic segment of the population and to every ethnic group. Including RFO, 25 radio stations operate in Tahiti. Many are commercial ventures reaching out to specific segments of the population, while some are run by the churches. The most popular is Radio 1, which features local and international news as well as French and international pop music. It also puts on musical concerts for its listeners every year. Tiare FM is 100-percent Polynesian, broadcasting in the Tahitian language and promoting local artists.

"The sad, weird, mysterious utterances of nature: the scarcely articulate stirrings of fancy... Faa-fano: the departure of the soul at death. Aa: happiness, earth, sky, paradise. Mahoi: essence or soul of God. Tapetape: the line where the sea grows deep. Tutai: red clouds on the horizon. Ari: depth, emptiness, a wave of the sea. Po: night, unknown dark world, Hell."

—Pierre Loti on the mystical vocabulary of Tahitian

TAHITIAN NAMES

In Tahitian society, a person's name is of utmost importance because it confers certain qualities on its bearer. An inanimate object, such as a musical instrument, may also be given a name in order to confer spiritual qualities on it.

In pre-Christian times, the chiefs' names were supposed to contain supernatural power that was beneficial to their descendants but brought a curse on their usurpers. The chiefs could also take on a name to mark an important event. In this way Tu, the first king of Tahiti, became Pomare after he visited his son who was sick with coughing. The words *po* (night) and *mare* (cough) became taboo once they were the king's name, and new words came into being to denote "night" and "cough."

There were no surnames in ancient Tahiti. The nobles used the name of their *marae* to denote their association with a certain clan. However, all Tahitian families now have surnames.

An ancient custom that is still in use today is for parents, grandparents, or other older relatives of importance in the family to give the married name to newlyweds, as well as choosing the names of their firstborn grandson and granddaughter. Nowadays many Tahitians have Western names such as John, David, or Rose.

Tahitian names are actually part of a phrase with a certain meaning. Some of them are descriptive of the qualities invested in the bearer, while others refer more to a state of being. Here are a few examples:

Eeva (f) from *Te-fetu-eeva-i-te-po*, meaning "The star that rises at night."

Marotea (m) from *Te-aito-maro-tea*, meaning "The hero with a white belt."

Moetu (f) from *Moe-tu-i-te-ara-nui*, meaning "Asleep standing on the highway."

Viritua (m) from *Viri-tua-i-te-moana-tapu*, meaning "Rolling beyond the sacred sea."

RFO also operates two television stations in Tahiti, one in French and the other in Tahitian. Most of the programs are imported from three stations in France and are current affairs programs, variety and game shows, and movies. RFO broadcasts from 5 A.M. to 1 A.M. daily. Set up with the help of the French Polynesian government in 2004, Tahiti Nui Television aims to promote and preserve Polynesian culture through its emphasis on local and regional news, sports, and music. The station offers a mixture of French programs, local news, and documentaries. Canal+, the French private satellite network, is also available in French Polynesia.

A man reading *Les Nouvelles de Tahiti* in a Papeete café.

ARTS

THE ARTS SCENE IN TAHITI has been dominated by a few European personalities. Yet Tahitians are an innately artistic people who treasure beauty in their daily lives, as demonstrated by the flower garlands and headdresses they love to weave and wear. Artistry is displayed in every small garden plot, where flowers are grown in harmonious beauty. Local Tahitian artists have produced noteworthy works of art that sadly remain overshadowed by works of European artists of old, such as Gauguin. In the arena of traditional artisan work, however, local Tahitian artists have made their mark. These include quilting and rug and basket weaving (particularly renowned in the Austral Islands), which are done by women. Wood carving by Tahitian male artists is much admired in the Marquesas.

Left: **Polynesian tattoos are striking and skilfully created. The traditional designs retain their popularity among Tahitian men.**

Opposite: **A brightly colored Tahitian sarong or cloth on display along a Tahitian beach.**

"Remember that you are not dancing by yourself. You are part of a group, and you should be aware of those who are around you so as to perform group movements."

—*Coco, director of Te Maeva dance group, to his dancers*

However, it is in the performing arts that Tahiti really comes into its own. Tahitian dancing has been elevated to a precise art form, and standards keep improving, with regular dancing competitions that are hotly contested. One should hope that as Tahitian society becomes more familiar to the rest of the world, other forms of artistic expression will gain as much recognition as dancing.

DANCING

The Tahitian term for dancing is *ori Tahiti* (oh-REE tah-hih-TIH), which means "Tahitian dancing in the traditional style." Another word commonly used to describe it is *tamure* (tah-MOO-ray).

Tahitian children are exposed to dancing from a young age. Most schools teach dancing as a recreational activity, and local parishes also have their own dance groups where children are introduced to this

PROFESSIONAL DANCE TROUPES

Until World War II, Tahitian dancing was considered immoral and was thus suppressed. Soon after the war, Madeleine Moua, an accomplished dancer, decided to give more dignity to dancing by forming the dance group Heiva I Papeete. Heiva was the first professional dance group in Tahiti, and the group is still very active. Today there are several other professional troupes in the country as well, each with 20–40 members. Normal performances, however, do not require more than eight female and four male dancers. Most professional dancers are around 20 years old. Physical requisites for men are average size, hair that falls at least to the shoulders, and no beard or mustache. Women dancers should ideally have a slim and graceful silhouette, a pleasant face, and long, dark hair, especially if they are performing for tourists. Height and size are important in *tamure* because group dancing requires uniformity. However, for community performances, the primary prerequisite for participation is youth.

ancient art form. Whereas the first missionaries viewed Tahitian dancing as obscene and sinful, the churches now promote it as a form of collective activity. Dance groups are formed at various levels, in church or regional groups. *Tamure* is almost exclusively dancing in a group. Even though a dance may include a solo performance, it is the group movements that create the beauty of the dance.

Vivid and colorful costumes add to the visual effect of a dance. There are basically two types of costumes: *more* (moh-RAY), which is a grass skirt, and pareu, the colorful length of cotton. The *more* is the more elaborate costume. It is accompanied by a variety of creative natural accessories such as a belt sewn with shells, flowers, and seeds; a garland of flowers or shells; a flower headdress; and a bra for the women dancers. These accessories vary greatly every year. Women sling the *more* low

Amateur or professional, Tahitians love to dance.

BASIC *TAMURE* MOVEMENTS

The basic step for men is the *paoti* (PAH-oh-tih). The legs are held close together with heels touching, feet pointing outward, and knees slightly bent. The knees then move outward and inward in a scissors motion while the heels come up slightly. Arms are stretched out horizontally, with the elbows straight and the fingers held together and pointing slightly upward. The rest of the body does not move at all.

For women, the starting position is the same as for men. The knees are then slightly raised, alternating between left and right, as if walking on the spot. Since the heels are still flat on the ground, this knee movement causes the hips to swing out from side to side. They are not supposed to twist forward. Arms are outstretched, as for men. It is essential that the shoulders and upper torso do not move.

"Before very long I am going to Tahiti. It's a little island in the Pacific where you can live without having to worry about money. I want to forget all the bad things that have happened and die over there without anyone here knowing. I want to be free to paint, as I am not interested in having a glorious reputation."

—Paul Gauguin

on the hips to accentuate the hip movements, while male dancers tie theirs at the waist. For special events, the flower headdress is replaced by a tall elaborate headgear made of fibers, and male dancers add a short cape to the costume. Dancers also hold in their hands a tuft of fibers that resemble longish pompoms, called *ii*. The pareu, on the other hand, is worn with only a garland and flowers in the hair.

Four types of dances are performed in Tahiti today: *otea*, *aparima*, *hivinau*, and *paoa*. The best-known and oldest is the *otea*, and Tahitians look upon it as a symbol of their culture.

OTEA   *Otea* (oh-TAY-ah) is performed for special events. For this reason, the dancers always wear the *more*. The larger the group of dancers, the more beautiful the dance is. *Otea* can bring together up to 60 dancers, and the minimum is six. The dancers form separate columns of men and women facing the spectators. They all move at the same time, and the formation remains the same throughout the performance. *Otea* is physically very demanding and does not last more than six minutes. A performance usually consists of a series of *otea* lasting about 15 minutes. When *otea* is danced by a group of men, it is a war dance, and the dancers often hold spears in their hands.

APARIMA   *Aparima* (AH-pah-ree-mah) is a narrative dance that is sometimes accompanied by a song. Dressed in pareus, the dancers are

These men are dancing at the Heiva i Tahiti festival. Such dramatic costumes are worn only for special events.

placed in the same column formation as for *otea*. At least six men and women are required for this dance. Depicting scenes from daily life, such as fishing or preparing food, the dancers use their hands to mime their actions. The emphasis is placed on the hand movements, and the *aparima* is usually performed in a kneeling position or in a sitting position with legs tucked underneath.

HIVINAU *Hivinau* (hee-vee-NOW) comes from the English term "heave now" used by the 19th-century English-speaking sailors when lifting anchor. It is essentially a party dance, and children and old people can join in. When performed for an audience, *hivinau* brings together a mixed group of around 20 male and female dancers dressed in *more*. The dancers form two circles, men and women separately, with a singer and a group of musicians in the middle. The two circles are in constant motion, moving in opposite directions or both in a clockwise direction. The male singer sings a few lines, and the dancers answer with "Ahiri a ha ahaha!" This phrase does not have any meaning—it is only a shout of joy. A common subject for *hivinau* is fishing and the sea.

PAOA *Paoa* (pah-OH-ah) originates from tapa-making sessions, when a group of women sat down to beat tree bark into tapa cloth, singing and beating at the same time. Today the subject of the dance is usually fishing or hunting. The *paoa* dance group consists of a male singer, a large choral group of men and women, musicians, and one or two dancers. Depending on the occasion, the group wears *more* or everyday clothes.

PAINTING

Almost from the moment Tahiti was discovered by Europeans, the island was the subject of many paintings by visitors who wanted to record its landscapes and people. The first painter to depict

Tahitian children learn to dance from a young age. Their movements and costumes are the same as those of adult dancers.

scenes of Tahiti was Englishman William Hodges, who was part of Cook's second expedition in 1773. He made pictorial records of the ship's landing and scenes of daily life and drew portraits of Tahitian people, including Omai and King Pomare. The 19th century attracted more painters in search of inspiration. While Frenchmen Paul

Gauguin and Jacques Boullaire were more interested in painting faces and expressions, Englishwoman C. F. Gordon Cumming painted beautiful watercolors depicting Papeete and other Tahitian landscapes.

Tahitian painting is no longer the domain of foreigners in search of exoticism. Several local painters have made a name for themselves through regular exhibitions, and the Association of Artists was created in 1984 to develop this art form. One of the best-known Tahitian painters is Ruy Juventin, who actively promotes local painting. Because there is no tradition of painting in Tahitian society, artists tend to follow European models, and there are a variety of styles in their productions. These variations help enrich Tahitian art through painting.

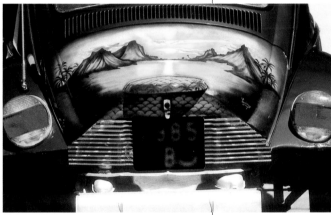

A painting of a sunset decorates the back of this car.

LITERATURE

Just like painting, writing about Tahiti has traditionally come from European and American authors. The first piece of writing about Tahiti was Bougainville's myth-making account of his visit to the island. About a century later, Pierre Loti (whose real name was Louis-Marie Julien Viaud) wrote *Le Mariage de Loti,* a sad love story about a young French navy lieutenant and a teenage *vahine.* The book was an instant success. Tahiti has also inspired much writing in English, including novels by Herman Melville (*Typee* and *Omoo*) and poetry by Rupert Brooke ("Tiare Tahiti").

PAUL GAUGUIN

Paul Gauguin was in a desperate financial situation when he arrived in Tahiti in 1891. He started out by painting the portraits of wealthy settlers in Papeete, but he soon grew tired of this and left Papeete for Mataiea.

It was in Mataiea that Gauguin painted his most famous canvases. He lived with a young *vahine* named Tehaamana, who was one of his favorite models. In this two-year period he produced 66 paintings, among them such masterpieces as *Ia Orana Maria, Hina Tefatou, Manao tupapau, Fatata te miti, Rêverie*, and *Under the Pandanus*.

Gauguin left Tahiti in 1893, hoping to sell his paintings in Paris. However, his exhibition of paintings of Tahitians caused a scandal. Then he started writing a book titled *Noa Noa*, in which he described life in Tahiti as a blissful existence. He returned to Tahiti in 1895, but he was plagued by financial and health problems, and his paintings took on a more pensive note. He died in the Marquesas in 1903, in abject poverty.

During his lifetime, Gauguin was treated harshly by the French government and settlers, and redress did not come until 1965, when the Gauguin Museum was opened in Papeari. The museum reconstructs Gauguin's life in Tahiti with the help of photographs and other objects. Unfortunately, none of his original paintings are displayed, since most of the painter's works are now exhibited at famous museums around the world.

Literature in the Tahitian language started only in the 1960s. It was written mainly by intellectuals in search of their cultural identity. Duro Raapoto is a linguist, poet, and fervent defender of the Tahitian language. His poems deal with the difficulties of life and reveal the aspirations of the Polynesian people. John Mairai uses theater to claim his Polynesian identity. His plays deal with the problems of daily life, and his caustic dialogues go down very well with his Tahitian audiences. Mairai was a friend of Henri Hiro, a prominent activist whose poetry sought to promote Polynesian culture in the 1970s and '80s.

CARVING

Ancient Tahitians carved plain, realistic figures, either as statues or as ornaments. Tikis are wooden or stone statues that had a religious significance. Petroglyphs are scenes carved out of stone, depicting stylized characters or objects such as fish, turtles, or headdresses. Articles for daily use as well as those for ornamental purposes were sculpted into decorative designs. Combs, handles of fans, and bowls were intricately carved out of wood, basalt, bone, and shell.

Today's artists use the same materials. Precious woods such as sandalwood, rosewood, and *tou* (toh-OO) are carved into weapons, tikis, and flat dishes. Basalt stone is best for pestles and adzes.

There are a number of other crafts to be found in Tahiti. Tahiti is well known for its basketwork. Pandanus leaves are woven into hats, baskets, and mats. Tahitian artisans are experts at making flower garlands and headdresses. Shells and coral are made into beautifully intricate jewelry.

Polynesian carvings are both stylized and expressive.

PATCHWORK QUILTS

An interesting craft in Tahiti is the two-layer patchwork quilt called *tifaifai* (tih-FAI-fai). Made of light cotton, it is the local adaptation of the quilting taught by missionaries. In the *tifaifai*, one large design is appliquéd onto the cotton base in bold color combinations, producing an unmistakably Tahitian look. Floral patterns and contrasting colors are preferred. The quilt is used to cloak newlyweds and cover coffins. A good one takes up to six months to complete. The making of *tifaifai* is solely the domain of women, and each woman has individual quilt patterns that are her trademarks. French painter Henri Matisse, who spent several weeks in Papeete, was so impressed by the *tifaifai* designs that he applied the same technique and adopted many designs for his paintings.

LEISURE

TAHITIANS BELIEVE THAT WORK is a necessary evil that must be done so that they can afford to enjoy themselves during their leisure time. They do not desire to gain more material wealth if they have to sacrifice their leisure activities for it.

Sports, dancing, and having fun play an important part in the Tahitians' daily lives. They prefer leisure activities that involve a group of people because Tahitian society was traditionally one of communal living. Getting together with a group of *fetii* (fay-tee-EE), even if only for a chat, is a source of great enjoyment. *Fetii* means "relatives," but the word is commonly used in a wider sense of close friends.

Together with these traditional activities, Tahitians spend a lot of time performing a very modern activity: watching television.

String instruments such as the guitar and the ukulele are an imported tradition. There are two local versions of the ukulele. One is a piece of wood glued to half of a coconut shell. The other is carved from a piece of wood with a length of goatskin covering the opening. Both have four nylon strings.

Left: **A young Tahitian man relaxes by playing a game of pool.**

Opposite: **Tahitian children take a carefree leap off a bridge into one of the many ponds and lakes that dot the country.**

A group of Tahitian musicians.

MUSIC

Music is in the blood of the Tahitian people. At home after work, they sometimes bring out a guitar or a ukulele and sing a few songs as a form of leisure activity. Groups of *fetii* meet on the weekend to sing and make music. Although they also play traditional Tahitian ballads, they prefer English-language pop songs. Nowadays it is common to bring along a portable stereo to provide the music while everyone sings along, chats, or drinks. No party or outing is complete without music.

Singing in Tahitian is called *himene*, from the English word "hymn." Indeed, the church is where most singing takes place. However, the word also refers to any form of group singing. *Himene* groups are usually formed on a regional basis, and anyone, young or old, can be a member. Singing is done while seated, with a male soloist leading the group. *Himene tarava* (hee-MAY-nay tah-RAH-vah) consists of a large number of men and women singing a cappella (without instrumental accompaniment) in 6–10 parts. It narrates ancient Tahitian legends or historical events. *Ute* (OO-tay) is less dignified: A group of men and women sing a refrain in a guttural voice while a soloist improvises a comic or satirical narration.

Himene groups also take part in some dances, such as *aparima* and *hivinau*. On these occasions, they sing to the accompaniment of musical instruments.

THE LURE OF WATER

Typical islanders, Tahitians love all activities related to water. Swimming is a favorite pastime, in rivers and the sea as well as under waterfalls. Picnics are very popular weekend outings because they combine family togetherness with the opportunity to go swimming. Favorite picnic places are the beach or an isolated *motu*.

Tahitians really come into their own when practicing water sports. Surfing is one of the oldest activities in Tahiti, having been documented by the first European visitors. Tahitian children do not need to go to the expense of buying fancy surfboards. They can ride the waves with anything at hand that is flat and light. The French national champions for surfing and windsurfing are usually Tahitians, and French surfers and windsurfers find that Tahiti is the ideal location in which to prepare for international competitions. Canoeing is another ancient sport: Tahitian canoes require several people to row, testing the team's strength, endurance, and sense of timing.

Swimmers and surfers enjoy Tahiti's clear water, mild weather, and clean beaches.

In many areas, especially in the countryside, a person's leisure time is dominated by church-related activities. Members of the choir get together for rehearsals, while others form committees to organize social gatherings such as celebratory dinners or dancing parties.

SPORTS

The most popular sport is soccer. Well before the colonizers introduced the game to the island, the ancient Tahitians played a game called *tuiraa* (too-ee-RAH-ah), which consisted of kicking a ball into the opponent's camp. Competition was fierce among the districts, and the game was as popular as soccer is today. Soccer matches take place on weeknights and weekends at several soccer fields, the more popular ones being Fautaua Stadium and Stade Pater, both in Pirae, near Papeete. Enthusiastic crowds cheer on their favorite teams. Other team sports, such as volleyball and basketball, are also very popular, especially among the lower-income groups. Games of *pétanque* (pay-TAHNK), or French bowling, take place in rural areas.

More expensive sports, practiced mainly by the wealthy Demis and Popaa, are tennis, golf, and horseback riding. Tennis courts are located mainly in the hotels and in Papeete as well as at private sports clubs. The Atimaono golf course was built on a former cotton plantation located between the lagoon and the mountains in a very colorful setting. There are two riding schools in Pirae that organize excursions into the mountains and the tropical forests.

Local spectator sports include Tahitian-style horse racing and cockfighting. Jockeys ride bareback, dressed in a brightly colored pareu and a flower headdress. Races are held on special occasions at the Pirae Hippodrome. Cockfighting, on the other hand, is illegal. However, fighting rings are out in the open, and the cockfights draw large crowds. Both horse racing and cockfighting take place on Sunday afternoons.

Sport fishing for marlin, shark, and other big game attracts many visitors to Tahiti. One of the most famous was U.S. novelist Zane Grey, who made several fishing expeditions to Tahiti in the 1920s. His determination was rewarded by the capture of a 1,000-pound (454-kg) marlin in 1930.

GAMBLING

Tahitians of all social backgrounds like to gamble. In addition to lotto, there is another popular lottery that is organized by various groups year-round—the French national lottery, or *tombolas* (tum-BOH-lah). Winning numbers for the *tombolas* are drawn from a revolving drum, large sums of money are risked, and the draw is eagerly awaited by all concerned. Horse racing also gives rise to betting through the official pari-mutuel, which offers bets on horse and greyhound racing through the fixed-odds system. Even though payoffs are quite small compared with those of the *tombolas*, betting on horse races is still popular. Serious betting is also done on the outcome of cockfights, although this is, of course, illegal.

Cocks bred for cock-fighting.

Tahitians like to spend a day at the races, particularly if they can place a bet on their favorite horse.

TAHITIAN DRUMS

The traditional Tahitian musical instrument is the drum. *Toere* (toh-AY-ray) is an unusual drum carved out of one piece of wood. It is basically a hollowed-out tree trunk with a rectangular slit running down the middle. The drummer holds it upright with one end on the floor and beats the side with a stick to produce a staccato beat. *Toere* come in three sizes, and each size produces a different sound. Some musicians name their *toere* in order to impart certain spiritual qualities to it or to distinguish it from others.

Faatete (fah-AH-tay-tay) is another ancient drum. It is made from a hollowed tree trunk covered with a skin, traditionally shark but today more commonly calf. The skin is stretched before each performance and loosened afterward. *Faatete* usually measure 25 inches (64 cm) in height and 12 inches (30 cm) in diameter. Decorative motifs are carved on the sides.

Pahu (pah-HOO) is of Western origin and can be made from wood or cut out from a metal barrel. To produce quality sound, the diameter and the height must be roughly the same: 20–30 inches (51–76 cm). The covering is of calfskin, and the *pahu* is decorated with paintings. The drum has two skins, but only one side is beaten with a stick. The drummer sometimes uses his hand to hit the other side. The musician is always seated with the *pahu* on its side in front of him.

Casino-style gambling takes place in various hotels and under the cover of charity evenings organized by the Lions Club or other charitable organizations. Patrons play roulette and blackjack in a secretive atmosphere. Games of Asian origin, such as "big and small," or *van lak,* are also played, mostly illegally. Keno, a type of lotto, draws large crowds.

However, Tahitians do not need any betting structure to gamble. Many weekends are spent playing cards for cash wagers. The contests during Heiva i Tahiti (Festival of Tahiti) give rise to the most widespread betting of the year.

BRINGUE

Bringue (BRAING) means "having a good time," drinking, singing, dancing. There is no specific activity called *bringue.* Weddings, parties, discos, and other celebrations are all *bringues.* Some rural districts organize their own Saturday night *bringue,* usually as a fund-raising activity.

The music and dancing at a *bringue* are most often of Western inspiration. Pop songs and disco-style dancing are the norm. Sometimes the songs are in Tahitian, but the music is Western. Tahitian music is also played,

Stone fishing taking place in the clear waters of Tahiti.

and people dance, but the participants do not do the traditional *tamure.* Instead couples face each other, the woman swinging her hips and the man opening and closing his knees. Young and old have fun at the *bringue.* Children sing and dance with their parents and grandparents, and the *bringue* often does not end until late into the night.

FESTIVALS

DESPITE ITS REPUTATION FOR BEING FUN-LOVING, Tahiti does not have many colorful festivals. Because of the far-reaching influence of the Evangelical Church, religious celebrations are marked with sobriety and do not give rise to the carnivalesque festivities common on the other islands.

The most remarkable festival is a political one, Heiva i Tahiti, which marks the country's accession to internal autonomy. The most popular activities during Heiva i Tahiti are the competitions of traditional and modern sports, dancing, and *himene*.

Tahiti has the same public holidays as France, but festivals include those of the other segments of the population, such as Chinese New Year and Tiare Tahiti Day, which honors Tahiti's national flower.

Above: **A canoe race during Heiva i Tahiti. Heiva i Tahiti, held every July, is celebrated with Polynesian dance, songs, and traditional sports.**

Opposite: **Young Tahitian men in traditional costumes made of leaves in celebration of a festival.**

HEIVA I TAHITI

The most important and colorful festival of the year is Heiva i Tahiti, which means simply "Festival of Tahiti." Festivities start on June 29, the Anniversary of Internal Autonomy, and culminate on Bastille Day, July 14, cleverly linking two directly opposing inspirations: the nationalism of the Tahitian people and the colonial dominance of France. The festival comes from the French national day festivities during colonial times. While the governor and French administrators celebrated the occasion with a ball and a state banquet, the Tahitians were entertained with traditional games and cultural performances. In 1984, when Tahiti was granted full internal autonomy, the pro-French president of the Territorial Assembly hit upon the idea of bringing the start of the festivities forward by a few days to June 29 and combining the internal-autonomy celebrations with those of Bastille Day.

The highlights of the Heiva festivities are most certainly the competitions among contestants from the various districts and the outer islands. Traditional competitions are canoe racing, javelin throwing, stone lifting, coconut husking, basket weaving, *tamure*, and *himene*. Canoe races for both men and women are fiercely contested, with teams coming from all over the world. The canoes are carved out of a single tree trunk, and the race covers 4 miles (6.5 km) along the Papeete waterfront. One unusual

CALENDAR OF FESTIVALS

January 1	New Year's Day
March 5	Missionaries Day
March–April	Good Friday
March–April	Easter Monday
May 1	May Day
May 8	Victory Day
May	Ascension Day
May–June	Whitsunday and Whitmonday
June 29	Anniversary of Internal Autonomy
June 29–July 14	Heiva i Tahiti
July 14	Bastille Day
August 15	Assumption Day
September 8	Internal Autonomy Day
November 1	All Saints' Day
November 11	Armistice Day
December 25	Christmas

event is the fruit-bearers' race. Male participants, dressed in pareus and flower headdresses, carry a colorful load of tropical fruits balanced on two ends of a banana tree trunk over a distance of 1.25 miles (2 km).

Less exotic competitions include bicycle, car, and horse races; *pétanque*; and archery contests. Traditional tattooing sessions bring together young people who want to experience their cultural heritage. *Bringues* are organized by regional organizations, and there is much dancing and feasting.

The Heiva celebrations also give rise to a festival of artisans. Palm-covered booths are crammed with the crafts of Polynesia. This is the largest gathering of craftspeople in French Polynesia. Hundreds of artisans gather to exhibit their artistry. Special events are held, including demonstrations of *tifaifai* quilting, weaving, and flower headdress making. The artisans dress in traditional attire, and there is always music and dancing.

July 2, which falls during the Heiva festival, evokes a totally different sentiment. This is the anniversary of the first French nuclear test at Moruroa in 1966, and commemorative ceremonies take place in Papeete.

BASTILLE DAY

Bastille Day on July 14 marks the end of the Heiva celebrations. France's national day, Bastille Day commemorates the storming of the Bastille prison on July 14, 1789, at the height of the French Revolution. It symbolizes the end of the tyranny of the kings and a new era of freedom and democracy for the French people.

In Tahiti, the streets are decorated with French and Tahitian flags, and a military parade takes place in Papeete. Speeches are made, the republic is toasted, and fireworks light up the night sky. An all-night ball, today's version of the governor's ball, attracts revelers on July 13 in Papeete.

One of the main events on Bastille Day is the military parade in Papeete.

Nowadays the military parade is losing its importance. Since Tahiti gained internal autonomy, attention has focused more on the parades of sports and cultural associations, which bring together *himene* groups, *tamure* troupes, and Chinese dancers, all dressed in their best finery.

RELIGIOUS FESTIVALS

The major Christian holidays are celebrated with fervor in Tahiti. Every Tahitian Christian attends church service, and the *himene* is even more beautiful on such occasions.

Christmas is certainly the most important religious holiday. However, this is a tropical Christmas. Flowers are in full bloom, and they decorate houses and churches. Many church organizations hold a *bringue* with food cooked in a traditional buried oven. Children polish their shoes so that *Père Noël* (pair noh-ELL), or Santa Claus, will leave presents in or on them.

Easter is ushered in by a late-night vigil. Some Catholics fast for 40 days, the duration of Lent, a period when Christians get ready spiritually for the miracle of the Resurrection. Mass is said on the three days preceding Easter, with reenactments of Jesus Christ's last actions before being crucified. Chocolate eggs and Easter bunnies are given to children.

On All Saints' Day, families spend the day cleaning the graves of all the cemeteries at Papeete, Faaa, Arue, and Punaauia and decorating them with fresh flowers. Flower stands are set up all over the island, and people light candles in the cemeteries.

Assumption Day is celebrated only by the Catholic community. It marks the assumption of the Virgin Mary to heaven. The church service pays special attention to children, for they are all considered children of Mary.

A special holiday in Tahiti is March 5—Missionaries Day or Gospel Day. It commemorates the arrival of Protestant missionaries in 1797. Protestant churches hold a special service. All government offices and most businesses are closed on that day.

Young Tahitians celebrating Tahiti's annual Evangile Festival in colorful festive clothes.

117

Tattooed Tahitian dancers performing a festive dance.

FAIRS

In addition to public holidays, there are a number of nonholiday fairs celebrating a flower or a region.

Taupiti O Papeete in May celebrates the town of Papeete. Miss Papeete is elected, and a carnival atmosphere reigns, with rides, games, and contests. The important activities take place on weekends.

The day honoring Tahiti's national flower, the *tiare Tahiti*, falls on December 2. A *tiare* is presented to everyone on the streets of Papeete, in the hotels, and at the airport. The highlight of this fair is an all-night ball with flowers decorating the ballroom, the tables, and even the performers.

CHINESE NEW YEAR

The Chinese community of Tahiti, together with all other Chinese populations worldwide, celebrates Chinese New Year in January or February. Based on the lunar calendar, Chinese New Year marks the arrival of spring in China and is thus a time of new beginnings and taking stock. The most important part of Chinese New Year is the reunion dinner on New Year's Eve. On this evening, the whole family gathers for a special dinner prepared with much care. Everyone makes it a point to be home early, and married children return to their parents' house for dinner. After the dinner, parents give *hong bao* (hong POW), red envelopes containing money, to the children.

A number of cultural performances are staged to mark Chinese New Year. Dances and fireworks are always on the program. Chinese businesses, especially grocery stores, remain closed for several days, as this is the only occasion during the year when the shopkeeper can take time off.

BEAUTY CONTESTS

Throughout the year, there is a proliferation of beauty contests attracting the most beautiful girls in Tahiti. The beauty contests are popular among young women, as there are prizes offered and the winner can enjoy the celebrity that comes with being elected Miss Tahiti or Miss Papeete.

Beauty queens are chosen to represent sports clubs, philanthropic associations, the Chinese community, and other groups. In addition, nightclubs in Papeete try to attract more customers by organizing regular beauty contests promoting a brand of beer or liquor or representing the nightclub. A Miss Heiva is elected in June, and she acts as a queen of the Heiva i Tahiti celebrations.

Male beauty contests are also common, and a Miss Raerae is chosen every year from the transvestite community. Aside from the Miss Raerae contests, there are other male beauty contests such as the Mr. Tahiti contest, which celebrates "masculine" beauty.

FOOD

TAHITIAN CUISINE MAKES USE of what nature provides in profusion: fish, fruits, and vegetables. However, aside from the staples such as breadfruit, taro, and bananas, most of the fruits and vegetables used in daily meals have been introduced only in the past two centuries. Coconut milk is used to flavor sauces, and coconut cream turns desserts into something special.

As a rule, Tahitian food is bland. Some dishes, especially such delicacies as raw fish and *popoi* (POH-poy), are an acquired taste. *Popoi*, a paste made from breadfruit, used to be the mainstay of the Tahitian diet but has now been replaced by the long loaf of French bread. Polynesians, Popaa, and Chinese alike eat baguettes at every meal. The reasons are both practical and economic. Bread does not require any preparation, and it is one of the most filling and least expensive items of food available. A typical Tahitian breakfast consists of bread, coffee, and perhaps some fruit.

The main meal of the day for the Popaa population is lunch, consisting of meat, potatoes, and bread, sometimes accompanied by wine. Dinner is very light, usually leftovers from lunch. For the Polynesians and the Chinese, on the other hand, dinner is the heaviest meal of the day.

Restaurants are plentiful in Papeete, offering French, American, Italian, Chinese, and Vietnamese cuisine. They tend to be expensive—few Polynesians can afford to go out to a restaurant. Instead Polynesians head for the food wagons near the harbor. These small vans appear at around 5:30 P.M. serving cheap and good dinners, kabobs, French fries, and grilled meats.

Above: **Open through the night, wagons serving food cater to hungry *bringue*-goers.**

Opposite: **Tahitians enjoy the glorious abundance of fresh seafood.**

121

FISH

The favorite protein of Tahitians is fish, despite the fact that beef in Tahiti is quite cheap and of high quality. Perhaps this is because fishing is free and fish can be caught by anyone. About 300 species of fish abound in Polynesian waters, but not all of them are edible. The armored soldier fish and the unicorn fish are prized by Tahitian gourmets. Sea bass and blue-spotted grouper release a wonderful aroma when grilled, while parrot fish, Napoleon fish, and jacks are best eaten raw.

Fish is eaten primarily in three ways: poached, grilled, and raw. Poaching is an easy way of cooking fish. Lagoon fish such as red mullet, grouper, sea bass, and jacks are cooked in a clear broth and drizzled with coconut milk before serving. For grilling, Tahitians traditionally use coral as fuel in addition to firewood. The fire is started with twigs and coconut husks, and small pieces of coral are placed on top. Once the coral pieces are hot and have turned brownish, the fish are placed directly on them for cooking. In addition to lagoon fish, mahimahi and tuna are grilled.

However, one of the most popular ways to consume fish is to eat it raw. The more conventional dish is a type of salad that contains tomatoes, carrots, and onions. The fish, preferably fresh tuna, is first soaked in salt water, then marinated in lime juice before being mixed with the salad vegetables and coconut milk. This dish is simply called *poisson cru* (pwa-son CROO), meaning "raw fish" in French.

Fafaru (fah-fah-ROO) requires a more intriguing preparation, and the Tahitian people are divided over its merits. Those who like it love it, while those who dislike it hate it intensely. Three or four fish are placed in an airtight coconut-shell container and covered with seawater. The fish are left to soak in the water for two to three days. The liquid is sieved through a fine cloth before being returned to the container, while the fish are thrown away. Fresh fish cut into cubes is then added to the liquid and left to marinate for at least six hours before the *fafaru* is ready for consumption. The marinating liquid lends a very pungent aroma to the dish, and it is definitely an acquired taste. Raw fish is eaten on Sundays, on special occasions, or when entertaining guests.

Above: **Breadfruit paste wrapped in palm leaves.**

Opposite: **Fresh fish is laid out for sale at the popular Papeete market.**

ALL-PURPOSE TREES

Called *uru* (OO-roo) in Tahitian, the breadfruit is probably the most useful tree in Tahiti. Ancient Polynesian legends tell of a man who turned himself into a breadfruit tree to save his family from famine. A single tree can produce fruit three times a year for 50 years, with as many as 300 fruits each time. The starchy, easily digested fruit is rich in vitamin B and carbohydrates. In ancient times, to preserve the fruit for long voyages

Tahitian food is eaten with the fingers, Chinese food with chopsticks, and Western food with knives and forks.

or to prevent famine, mashes were prepared; to make *mahi* (mah-HEE), fragments of pulp were cooked after they had been left to ferment in a trench covered with leaves and soil. The trunk of the breadfruit tree was hollowed into small outrigger canoes, the bark was beaten into tapa, and the latex was used as a glue for capturing birds. The latex is still used today as a plaster for healing fractures, sprains, and rheumatic joints.

The coconut palm is another multipurpose tree. Like the breadfruit tree, it provides shade and decorates the landscape. The edible parts are the nut and the heart of the young sprout. The heart is very tender and can be eaten as a salad. The nut provides coconut water and coconut milk. The husk can be plaited or twisted into a rope and provides an ocher dye for all kinds of decoration. The flesh (copra), when dried, is squeezed for oil, which is used to make scented skin oil, perfumes, and soaps. The palm fronds are woven into mats, hats, baskets, and roofs. The ribs are used for making skewers and brooms. The trunk of the

FISH POISONING

Ciguatera is a type of food poisoning resulting from the consumption of toxic tropical fish. The fish themselves are poisoned by the *Gambierdiscus toxicus* (G.T.) toxin, which is associated with algae growing on dead coral. The most frequently affected species are sea perch, emperors, groupers, parrot fish, Napoleon fish, and triggerfish—all of which unfortunately form part of the Tahitians' staple diet. Deep-sea fish such as tuna, bonito, and mahimahi are never toxic. Every year around 1,000 people become victims of ciguatera in French Polynesia.

Ciguatera manifests itself in various symptoms, including a tingling sensation in the face and hands, vomiting, and diarrhea. The body feels weak, and the victim aches all over. Itching also occurs on the palms of the hands and the soles of feet, and for this reason, ciguatera is also known as "the itch." Severe cases can lead to death. However, normal cases of ciguatera are easily treated, and the symptoms subside after a few days.

coconut palm is sometimes used as building material, while the bark and the roots become ingredients of traditional remedies.

STAPLES

The traditional staple foods in the Tahitian diet are breadfruits, taros, *fei* (fay-EE) bananas, yams, and sweet potatoes. They are usually boiled or grilled and are eaten with fish and meats. *Fei* bananas are small, sweet, and red and must be cooked before being eaten.

Breadfruit is the most common staple. It is cooked whole over a wood fire, then peeled and eaten. A variation is to put the cooked breadfruit in a breadfruit leaf and hit it to form a paste. The breadfruit paste is then dipped into warm coconut milk before it is eaten. Breadfruit is also used to prepare *popoi*, another type of mash. The fruit is grated and wrapped in leaves before being boiled in water. Once cooked, the leaves are peeled off, lime juice and water are added, and the breadfruit is pounded for a while. *Popoi* is ready when the paste becomes elastic, and it is eaten with mashed bananas.

THE TAHITIAN OVEN

The Tahitian *ahimaa* (ah-hee-MAH-ah) is reserved for feasts called *tamaaraa* (tah-MAH-ah-RAH-ah), the equivalent of the Hawaiian luau, and can feed at least 30 people. More than a simple banquet, the preparation and eating of these feasts are an exercise in communal living. Men dig the pit while women wrap the food to be cooked.

Preparing an *ahimaa* with pork and breadfruit wrapped in palm leaves.

125

The pit is 9 feet (2.7 m) long, 2 feet (61 cm) wide, and 1 foot (30.5 cm) deep. It is dug at around noon or even the day before in order for the food to be ready by dinnertime. Dry branches and twigs are used to cover the bottom. Basalt stones are then placed on top of the branches, and a fire is lit in the pit. When the stones are red-hot, green branches and a layer of green banana leaves are spread over the stones, and the food is placed on top of the leaves. The whole pit is then covered with several layers of banana leaves, wet sacking, and sand. The *ahimaa* is left to bake for three hours.

The foods that go into the oven are wrapped separately in banana leaves so that they retain their individual flavors: suckling pig, fish, crayfish, crawfish, shrimp, *fafa* (fah-FAH)—chopped bits of chicken cooked with the tops of taro greens and coconut milk—a type of dessert called *poe* (poh-AY), breadfruit, sweet potato, taro, and *fei* bananas. Everything is eaten with the fingers off banana leaves, accompanied by a coconut-milk sauce fermented with the juice of river shrimp. In addition to the *ahimaa*, *fafaru* and *popoi* are eaten at the *tamaaraa*. Drinks include beer, red wine, and water.

A *tamaaraa* is always accompanied by music. The band is usually made up of guitars, a ukelele, and a unique instrument made of a gasoline can tied to a broomstick with a piece of string. Participants wear flowers in their hair, and colorful flowers decorate the banquet table and surroundings. The *tamaaraa* is a perfect occasion for family and friends to gather in a convivial atmosphere.

TAHITIAN DRINKS

The ancient Tahitians used a rather interesting method to make an intoxicating drink. Fresh kava roots were chewed, usually by women, and the saliva-covered roots were then diluted in water to produce a type of liquor.

Beer is the most popular drink. The traditional Tahitian beer was made with fruit juices (orange or pineapple) to which water and sugar were added. It was bottled and left to ferment for four to five days,

Above: **The refreshing water inside a young coconut is reached by chopping open the end of the coconut with a machete.**

Opposite: **A bunch of taro. The root of the taro can only be eaten cooked.**

The texture of cooked breadfruit resembles that of fresh bread rolled up into a semifirm mass.

TAHITIAN VANILLA

Used as a flavoring mainly in cooking and confectionery, vanilla also goes into the manufacture of perfumes and as a fragrance to mask the strong smell of rubber tires, paint, and cleaning products. Erroneously called a bean, it is actually the fruit of an orchid, the only edible one in the world.

When harvested, the beans have no smell. It takes several months of curing and processing for them to develop their distinctive aroma. Every 9 pounds (4 kg) of raw beans yield 2 pounds (1 kg) of vanilla. As vanilla is one of the world's most labor-intensive crops, it fetches a high price on the world market, especially in the years when the major producers are struck by storms.

Tahitian vanilla is different from the regular variety commonly available in the market (bourbon vanilla). As the Tahitian variety contains less vanillin (the substance that gives the vanilla its distinctive fragrance), the vanilla smell is less strong. However, it is more aromatic, with different undertones. It is therefore prized for its depth, subtlety, and nuances. Whereas bourbon vanilla is used mostly in industrial preparations, Tahitian vanilla is the flavor of choice for upscale restaurants and confectioners. Most of the vanilla essence on supermarket shelves is synthetic, and in fact, 97 percent of vanilla used in flavoring is synthetic.

The Tahitian government intends to capitalize on the high regard for Tahitian vanilla by offering economic incentives to producers and farmers. Initially grown mainly on the Leeward Islands, vanilla is set to spread to the rest of the archipelago, especially Tahiti. The main consumers of Tahitian vanilla are France, the United States, and Japan.

Tahitians enjoy a delicious dessert called poe. *It is a pudding made with tapioca flour and baked banana, papaya, or pumpkin. The flour and the fruit are mixed with coconut cream and flavored with vanilla.*

which caused the fizz in the drink. Today the local brewery produces a brand of European-style beer called Hinano from imported hops (a flower used to flavor beer), malt, and yeast. Only the water is Tahitian. Beer is considered a social drink because it is refreshing and inexpensive. It is always present during a gathering of *fetii*, and no *bringue* or *tamaaraa* is complete without it.

The most refreshing drink of all is undoubtedly fresh coconut water. It is the cheapest drink, after tap water. However, it is important to choose young fruits, which have sweet water. Once the nut has hardened, the water turns sour.

PAPEETE MARKET

Le marché (luh mar-SHAY), as Papeete's market is known, is housed in pretty new buildings located just one block from the waterfront. It is clean and free of unpleasant odors. Everything is available:

bread, fish, meat, fruit, vegetables, coconut-oil soap, tikis, and pareus. The market reflects an earlier Papeete—earthy, vibrant, colorful, and full of amiable confusion.

The market is most crowded between 5 A.M. and 8 A.M. on Sundays. The arrival of fresh fish at 5 A.M. and 4 P.M. marks the height of activity. Most of the market stallholders come from outside Papeete, and they arrive in trucks at about 4 A.M. Many vegetable and fruit sellers come from the outer islands, and they stay in Papeete until all their stock is sold. Some stay with *fetii*, but most sleep in the large covered hall next to the market. In the evening, the hall is transformed into a huge municipal dormitory when the visitors spread out their mats for the night.

The market is the heart of Papeete. Always bustling with activity and of-fering fresh produce, it is the favorite meeting place of Papeete residents and of outer islanders.

RAW FISH SALAD

2 pounds fresh tuna	3 small green onions
1 clove garlic, crushed	Juice from 8 limes
2 carrots	Milk squeezed from 1 grated coconut
1 small cucumber	Salt and pepper
2 tomatoes	Fresh bread cubes (optional)

Dice the tuna into bite-size pieces. Rinse the fish in salted water. Add the garlic, pour more salted water to cover the fish, and leave to marinate for 30 minutes in the refrigerator. Grate the carrots and cucumber. Slice the tomatoes and onions finely. Drain the salted water, pour in the lime juice with the fish, and leave to marinate for another five minutes. Discard lime juice. Stir in the vegetables and coconut milk. Season with salt and pepper. Mix well and serve cold. Fresh bread cubes can be tossed in the salad too.

FIRIFIRI

Firifiri is a doughnut in a figure-eight shape covered with powdered sugar. It is sold at markets and roadside stalls and eaten for breakfast or as a snack with a cup of coffee.

3 cups flour
1 package dry yeast
1½–2 cups water
1 cup sugar
Peanut oil for frying
Powdered/icing sugar

Mix the flour and the dry yeast with a spoon in a large bowl. Add the water, and mix thoroughly with a whisk to form a soft dough. Add sugar to taste, and leave to rise for four to five hours. Cover with a damp cloth. Cut the dough into midsize pieces, then pull and twist them to form figure eights. Fry in very hot peanut oil until golden. Roll the *firifiri* in powdered sugar and serve.

Point Venus

Mahina

Matavai Bay

Papenoo

Pirae

Arue

Vaimahuta

PAPEETE

Tiarei

Fautaua

Mahaena

Faaa

Tuauru

Papenoo

HITIAA O TE RA COMMUNE

Tahiti Nui

Mount Orohena
(7,337 ft / 2,235 m)
▲

Hitiaa

Fautaua

Mount Diademe
▲

Punaauia

Punaruu

Vaituoru

Mount Urufa
▲

Faaone

▲
Lake Vaihiria

Paea

Mount Tetufera

Taravao

Vairei

Isthmus of Taravao

Tautira

TEVA I UTA COMMUNE

Papeari

TAIARAPU EAST

Papara

Atimaono

Teohatu

Vaitepiha COMMUNE

Mataiea

Tahiti Iti (Taiarapu)

TAIARAPU

Vairao

▲ Mount Roniu

WEST

COMMUNE

P A C I F I C

Teahupoo

O C E A N

Pari Coast

MAP OF TAHITI

Arue, B1

Atimaono, B3

Faaa, A2

Faaone, C2

Fautaua, A2

Fautaua River,
   A1–A2, B2

Fautaua Valley,
   A1–A2, B2

Hitiaa, C2

Hitiaa O Te Ra
   Commune, C2

Isthmus of Taravao,
   C3

Lake Vaihiria, B2

Mahaena, C2

Mahina, B1

Mataiea, B3

Matavai Bay, B1

Mount Diademe, B2

Mount Orohena, B2

Mount Roniu, D3

Mount Tetufera, B2

Mount Urufa, B2

Pacific Ocean,
   A1–A4, B1–B4,
   C1–C4, D1–D4

Paea, A3

Papara, B3

Papeari, C3

Papeete, A2

Papenoo, B1

Papenoo River,
   B1–B2

Papenoo Valley,
   B1–B2

Pari Coast, D4

Pirae, A1

Point Venus, B1

Punaauia, A2

Punaruu River, A2,
   B2

Punaruu Valley, A2,
   B2

Tahiti Iti, C3–C4,
   D3–D4

Tahiti Nui, A2, B2

Taiarapu East
   Commune, C3,D3

Taiarapu West
   Commune, C3–
   C4, D3–D4

Taravao, C3

Tautira, D3

Teahupoo, D4

Teohatu, C3

Teva I Uta
   Commune, B3, C3

Tiarei, C2

Tuauru River, B1–
   B2

Tuauru Valley,
   B1–B2

Vaimahuta
   Waterfalls, B1–B2

Vairao, C3

Vairei, C3

Vaitepiha River, D3

Vaitepiha Valley, D3

Vaituoru, B2

ECONOMIC TAHITI

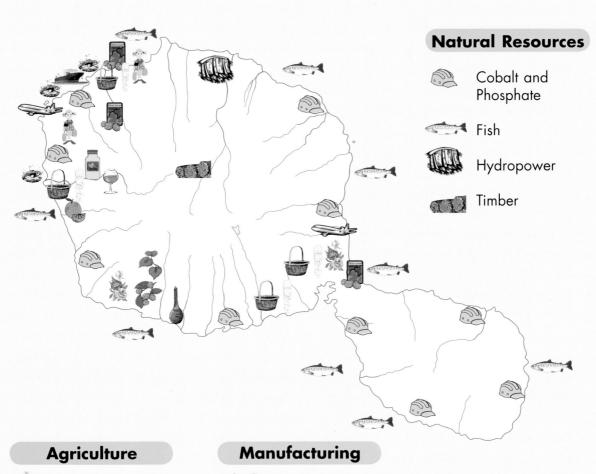

Natural Resources

- Cobalt and Phosphate
- Fish
- Hydropower
- Timber

Agriculture

- Flowers
- Kava
- *Noni*
- Oranges
- Vegetables

Manufacturing

- Arts and Crafts
- Beer and Wine
- *Noni* Juice
- Pearls
- Vanilla

Services

- Airport
- Sea Port
- Tourism

ABOUT THE ECONOMY

OVERVIEW
Since the end of the French nuclear program in the Pacific, Tahiti has moved toward greater economic self-sufficiency. Instead of supporting the military, funds from France are channeled into investment projects with long-term development. The challenge for the French Polynesian government is to share the newly created wealth with the other islands in the archipelago.

GROSS DOMESTIC PRODUCT (GDP)
$4.58 billion (2003 estimate)

GDP GROWTH
5.1 percent (2002 estimate)

LAND USE
Arable land 0.75 percent, permanent crops 5.5 percent, others 93.75 percent (2005 estimates)

INFLATION RATE
1.1 percent (2006 estimate)

CURRENCY
French Pacific franc (XPF)
Notes: 500, 1,000, 5,000, and 10,000 XPF
Coins: 1, 2, 5, 10, 20, 50, and 100 XPF
1 USD = 95.89 XPF (2006)

MINERAL RESOURCES
Cobalt, phosphate

AGRICULTURAL PRODUCTS
Coconuts, vanilla, vegetables, fruits, coffee, poultry, beef, dairy products

MAJOR EXPORTS
Tourism 34 percent, fish 31 percent, cultured pearls 26.5 percent

MAJOR IMPORTS
Fuels 16 percent, foodstuff 18.5 percent, machinery 32 percent

MAIN TRADE PARTNERS
France 52.7 percent, Singapore 14.9 percent, New Zealand 6.8 percent, United States 6.6 percent (2005 estimates)

WORKFORCE
65,930 (2005 estimate)

UNEMPLOYMENT RATE
11.7 percent (2005 estimate)

EXTERNAL DEBT
$7 million (2003 estimate)

CULTURAL TAHITI

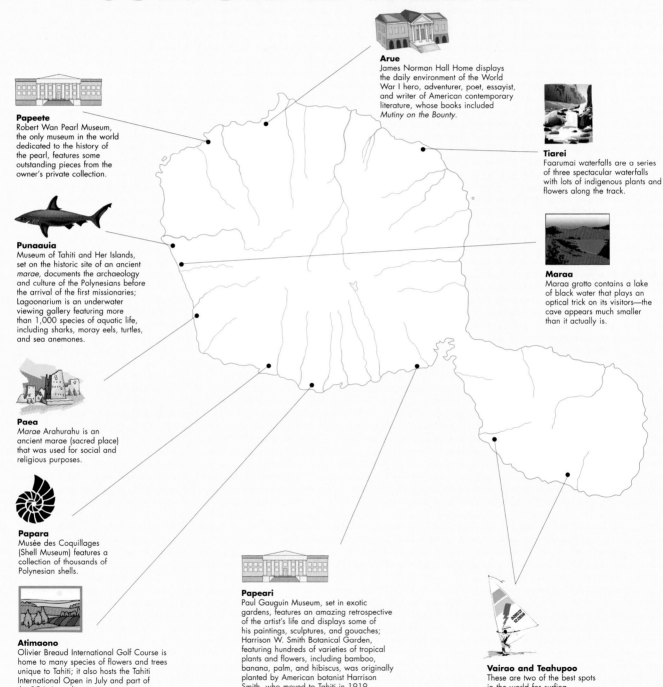

Arue
James Norman Hall Home displays the daily environment of the World War I hero, adventurer, poet, essayist, and writer of American contemporary literature, whose books included *Mutiny on the Bounty.*

Papeete
Robert Wan Pearl Museum, the only museum in the world dedicated to the history of the pearl, features some outstanding pieces from the owner's private collection.

Tiarei
Faarumai waterfalls are a series of three spectacular waterfalls with lots of indigenous plants and flowers along the track.

Punaauia
Museum of Tahiti and Her Islands, set on the historic site of an ancient *marae*, documents the archaeology and culture of the Polynesians before the arrival of the first missionaries; Lagoonarium is an underwater viewing gallery featuring more than 1,000 species of aquatic life, including sharks, moray eels, turtles, and sea anemones.

Maraa
Maraa grotto contains a lake of black water that plays an optical trick on its visitors—the cave appears much smaller than it actually is.

Paea
Marae Arahurahu is an ancient marae (sacred place) that was used for social and religious purposes.

Papara
Musée des Coquillages (Shell Museum) features a collection of thousands of Polynesian shells.

Atimaono
Olivier Breaud International Golf Course is home to many species of flowers and trees unique to Tahiti; it also hosts the Tahiti International Open in July and part of the PGA Australia circuit.

Papeari
Paul Gauguin Museum, set in exotic gardens, features an amazing retrospective of the artist's life and displays some of his paintings, sculptures, and gouaches; Harrison W. Smith Botanical Garden, featuring hundreds of varieties of tropical plants and flowers, including bamboo, banana, palm, and hibiscus, was originally planted by American botanist Harrison Smith, who moved to Tahiti in 1919.

Vairao and Teahupoo
These are two of the best spots in the world for surfing.

ABOUT THE CULTURE

OFFICIAL NAME
Overseas Lands of French Polynesia

FLAG DESCRIPTION
Two narrow red horizontal bands with a white band in between. A stylized red, blue, and white ship rides on a blue-and-white wave pattern in the middle of the white band, with a gold-and-white ray pattern above.

TOTAL AREA
402 square miles (1,041 sq km) land, Tahiti; 1,545,007 sq miles (4,001,550 sq km), French Polynesia

CAPITAL
Papeete

POPULATION
274,578 (2006 estimate)

BIRTHRATE
16.68 births per 1,000 Tahitians (2006 estimate)

DEATH RATE
4.69 deaths per 1,000 Tahitians (2006 estimate)

AGE STRUCTURE
0 to 14 years: 26.1 percent; 15 to 64 years: 67.9 percent; 65 years and over: 6.1 percent (2006 estimates)

ETHNIC GROUPS
Tahitians 65 percent, Demis (people of mixed parentage) 16 percent, Chinese 5 percent, Popaa (white, mainly French) 12 percent

RELIGIOUS GROUPS
Protestant 54 percent, Roman Catholic 30 percent, Church of Jesus Christ of the Latter-Day Saints (Mormons) 6 percent, Seventh-Day Adventist 2 percent, Buddhist, Jewish, and others 8 percent

MAIN LANGUAGES
French, Tahitian

LITERACY RATE
98 percent (1977 estimate)

NATIONAL HOLIDAYS
Anniversary of Internal Autonomy (June 29), Bastille Day (July 14), Internal Autonomy Day (September 8)

LEADERS IN POLITICS
King Pomare II (1774–1821), converted Tahiti to Christianity; Queen Pomare IV (1813–77), handed Tahiti over to the French government; Pouvanaa a Oopa, father of Tahitian nationalism (1895–1977); Oscar Temaru, first pro-independence president (b. 1944)

TIME LINE

IN TAHITI	IN THE WORLD
	753 B.C. Rome is founded.
c. 600 First settlement of Tahiti.	
1767 Discovery of Tahiti by Samuel Wallis, who claims the island for the British crown.	**1530** Beginning of transatlantic slave trade organized by the Portuguese in Africa
1768 Louis-Antoine de Bougainville visits Tahiti and claims the island for France, calling it New Cythera.	
1769 James Cook spends three months at Matavai observing the transit of Venus.	**1776** U.S. Declaration of Independence
1788 William Bligh of the HMS *Bounty* arrives in Tahiti.	
1790 Pomare I conquers all of Tahiti and becomes the first king.	**1789–99** The French Revolution
1812 Pomare II renounces the ancient Polynesian religion and converts to Christianity.	
1827 Pomare III dies suddenly. His sister becomes Queen Pomare IV and rules for 50 years.	
1834 Arrival of French missionaries	
1835 French Catholic missionaries are expelled from Tahiti.	
1842 French protectorate is proclaimed over Tahiti and Moorea.	
1844–46 The French–Tahitian War is fought.	
1847 Queen Pomare accepts French protectorate.	**1861** The U.S. Civil War begins.
1866 Introduction of French legislation	

IN TAHITI	IN THE WORLD
	1869 The Suez Canal is opened.
1880 The protectorate becomes a French colony.	
1885 Tahiti and the other islands in the archipelago become the Établissements Français de l'Océanie (French Oceania).	
1891 Paul Gauguin arrives in Tahiti and dies in 1903 on Hiva Oa.	
1914 Papeete is shelled by two German cruisers on September 22.	**1914** World War I begins.
1941–45 300 Tahitian volunteers fight in World War II.	**1939** World War II begins.
1942 American military base is established on Bora Bora.	**1945** The United States drops atomic bombs on Hiroshima and Nagasaki.
	1949 The North Atlantic Treaty Organization (NATO) is formed.
1984 Tahiti is granted full internal autonomy.	**1991** Breakup of the Soviet Union
	1997 Hong Kong is returned to China.
	2001 Terrorists crash planes in New York, Washington, D.C., and Pennsylvania.
2003 Tahiti changes its status to Collectivité d'outre-mer (French overseas community).	**2003** War in Iraq begins.
2004 Election of Oscar Temaru to the presidency; he is ousted later in the same year through a no-confidence vote by the assembly of French Polynesia; Tahiti becomes a *pays d'outre-mer*.	
2005 Oscar Temaru is reelected president.	

GLOSSARY

Afa Tahiti (AH-fah tah-hih-TIH)
Children of European and Polynesian parents

ahimaa (ah-hee-MAH-ah)
Food baked in an underground oven

breadfruit
A staple in the Tahitian diet; eaten boiled or grilled, the fruit has the taste and texture of bread

bringue (BRAING)
Party with singing, dancing, and drinking; literally, "having a good time"

Demis (doh-MEE)
Descendants of early marriages between Polynesians and Europeans

fafaru (fah-fah-ROO)
Raw fish marinated in seawater

fetii (fay-tee-EE)
Relatives, close friends

himene (hee-MAY-nay)
Singing; from the English word "hymn"

hombo (HOM-boh)
Delinquent who glorifies outlaws and comic-book characters

hupe (HOO-pay)
Mountain wind

Le truck (luh TRUCK)
Minibus used for public transport

maraamu (mah-rah-AH-moo)
Strong wind blowing from the southeast

marae (mah-RAH-ay)
Ancient place of worship

motu (moh-TOO)
Small island

Popaa (poh-pah-AH)
A white person, usually a French person; literally, "foreigner"

popoi (POH-poy)
Breadfruit paste eaten with coconut milk

raau tahiti (rah-AH-oo tah-hih-TIH)
Traditional Tahitian natural remedies

Taata Maohi (tah-AH-tah mah-OH-hee)
Name by which Polynesian Tahitians refer to themselves; literally, "people of Polynesia"

tahua (tah-HOO-ah)
Traditional healer

tamaaraa (tah-MAH-ah-RAH-ah)
Large feast of *ahimaa*

tamure (tah-MOO-ray)
Tahitian dancing

tiki
A carved figure or image representing an ancient Polynesian god

Tinito (tee-NEE-toh)
Chinese

vahine (vah-HEE-nay)
Woman

FURTHER INFORMATION

BOOKS

Barbieri, Gian Paolo. *Tahiti Tattoos*. Cologne: Benedikt Taschen Verlag, 1998.

Bolyanatz, Alexander. *Pacific Romanticism: Tahiti and the European Imagination*. Westport, CT: Praeger Publishers, 2004.

Loti, Pierre. *Tahiti: The Marriage of Loti*. London: Kegan Paul New Editions, 2002.

Nicole, Robert. *The Word, the Pen, and the Pistol: Literature and Power in Tahiti*. New York: State University of New York Press, 2000.

Peterson, Austin. *Tahiti Report: An In-Depth, Very Intimate Look at Tahiti Before the Jets Came (1960) and Today (2000)*. New York: Writers Club Press, 2000.

Prince, Jan. *Tahiti and French Polynesia Guide*. New York: Open Road Publishing, 2005.

Shackelford, George and Claire Freches-Thory. *Gauguin Tahiti*. Boston: MFA Publications, 2004.

WEB SITES

Agence Tahitienne de Presse. www.tahitipresse.pf

CIA World Factbook. www.cia.gov/library/publications/the-world-factbook/index.html (select "French Polynesia" from list of countries)

Presidency of French Polynesia. www.presidence.pf

Tahiti.com. www.tahiti.com

The Tahiti Traveler. www.thetahititraveler.com

World InfoZone. www.worldinfozone.com/country.php?country=FrenchPolynesia

FILMS

Cousteau: Tahiti–Fire Waters. Atlanta, GA: Turner Home Entertainment, 1998.

Mutiny on the Bounty. Hollywood: MGM, 1962.

Tahiti: French Polynesia. Huntsville, TX: Educational Video Network, Inc., 2006.

MUSIC

Heart of Tahiti. Gnp Crescendo, 1999.

Magic of the South Seas. Arc Music, 2000.

Tahiti Dances to Drums of Bora Bora and Papeete. Hana Ola Records, 2004.

BIBLIOGRAPHY

Andersen, Johannes C. *Myths and Legends of the Polynesians.* Mineola, NY: Dover, 1995.

Heyerdahl, Thor and F. H. Lyon. *Kon-Tiki: Across the Pacific by Raft.* Washington Program, 1995.

Howard, Michael. *Gauguin.* London: Dorling Kindersley, 1993.

Moorehead, Alan. *Fatal Impact: An Account of the Invasion of the South Pacific 1767–1840.* Mutual Publishing, 1989.

Putigny, Bob. *Tahiti and Its Islands.* Singapore: Les Editions du Pacifique, 1985.

Saquet, Jean-Louis. *The Tahiti Handbook.* Papeete: Editions Avant et Après, 1998.

Moruroa e tatou (association of veterans and victims of nuclear testing). www.moruroaetatou.org

Tahiti 1. www.tahiti1.com

INDEX

administrative districts, 12
agriculture, 10, 28, 42, 43–45
airport, 8, 11, 38, 46, 67, 118
ancient Polynesians, 20
ancient Tahitian explanation for the creation of the world, 85
ancient Tahitian social classes, 21
archipelagoes, 7–17, 37, 56–57
  Austral Islands, 7, 34, 37, 95
  Gambier Islands, 7, 44
  Marquesas Islands, 7
  Society Islands, 7, 87
  Tuamotu Islands, 7, 36
arts, 95–103
  crafts, 103, 115
  dancing, 96–100, 105, 111

music, 49, 67, 91, 93, 106, 111, 115, 127
  painting, 100–101
Arue, 11, 13, 38, 59, 117
Asia, 20, 36, 46, 57, 60, 128
assembly of French Polynesia, 33–35
atolls, 7, 9, 38, 39, 55
autonomy, 20, 30, 31, 33, 37, 113, 114, 116

banks, 12
basalt, 11,103
beaches, 9,10,51,107
beauty contests, 119
biodiversity, 51
Bora Bora, 28, 48, 57, 85
buildings, 12, 69, 70, 81, 128

businesses, 8, 12, 46, 67, 68, 117, 119

calendar of festivals, 114
canoes, 16, 20, 23, 46, 107, 110, 114, 124
Captain James Cook, 16, 73
carving, 102–103
children, 56, 60, 111, 116
citrus fruits, 43
civilization, 19
civil service, 35
cliffs, 8
climate, 13, 53
  rain, 13, 14
  temperatures, 13
coffee, 14, 121, 131
colonization, 19, 62, 69
constitution, 33

consumerism, 41
copra, 43, 46, 124
coral reefs, 7, 9, 15, 51, 52, 53, 85, 103, 122, 124
cost of living, 42, 67
Crook, James, 11
currency, 42

deforestation, 51–52
diseases, 17, 19, 24, 73
drinking water, 51
drinks, 127–128

Easter Island, 7, 87
economy, 41–49
education, 31, 33, 35, 57, 68, 71–72, 73, 79, 89
  compulsory education, 73
  curriculum, 71–72
  universities, 72
elections, 30, 31, 34, 36
electricity, 11
environment, 51–57
  conservation, 51
  ecological practices, 54
  environmental education, 57
  marine environment, 51, 52–55
  nuclear tests, 55–56
  rules and regulations, 55
  treatment of sewage, 51
  waste management, 57
  water pollution, 51
Établissements Français de l'Océanie, 29, 30
ethnicity
  Chinese, 28, 29, 59, 62–63, 67, 68, 69, 77, 87, 113, 116, 119, 121, 124
  Demi, 61, 62, 63, 64, 67, 68, 69, 87, 108
  European, 19, 23, 24, 26, 34, 46, 59, 61, 62, 64, 68, 74, 75, 82, 95, 101, 107, 128
  Polynesian, 7, 13, 17, 19, 21, 24, 26, 30, 36, 41, 42, 46, 51, 52, 53, 54, 55, 56, 57, 59, 60, 61, 62, 63, 64, 69, 71, 72, 74, 75, 79, 84, 85, 87, 89, 91, 93, 95, 102, 103, 113, 122, 123
  Popaa, 63, 64, 67, 68, 69, 80, 108, 121

Europe, 46, 62
European explorers, 19, 26, 59, 75
expedition, 19, 100

Faaa, 8, 11, 13, 38, 46, 49, 69, 72, 88, 117
fairs, 118
farmers, 22, 61, 67, 68, 69, 128
fauna, 16–17
  birds, 16, 17, 48, 124
  turtles, 17, 103
Fautaua, 16, 108
festivals, 113–119
  All Saints' Day, 114, 117
  Bastille Day, 113, 114, 115, 116, 117
  Chinese New Year, 113, 119
  Christmas Day, 116
  Easter Day, 7, 20, 29, 87, 114, 116, 117
  Heiva i Tahiti, 99, 111, 113, 114, 115, 119
  Missionaries Day, 114, 117
  Tiare Tahiti Day, 113
fish, 16, 17, 24, 41, 45, 46, 48, 49, 53, 54, 55, 69, 71, 84, 85, 103, 110, 121, 122, 123, 124, 125, 126, 129, 130
fishermen, 22, 48
fishing, 19, 41, 48–49, 54, 61, 99, 100, 108, 110, 111, 122
flora, 14–15, 54
flower garlands, 75, 95, 103
food, 121–131
  breadfruit, 25, 82, 121, 123, 124, 125, 126, 127
  fish, 122–123
  staples, 125
  taros, 125
foreign affairs, 35
forests, 14, 15, 51, 52, 54, 108
France, 24, 26, 28, 29, 30, 33, 34, 35, 36, 39, 41, 42, 45, 46, 47, 51, 55, 56, 59, 67, 69, 70, 71, 77, 78, 80, 81, 91, 93, 113, 115, 128
French civil servants, 34, 36, 42, 67
French government, 20, 26, 33, 38, 39, 42, 43, 47, 48, 56, 61, 63, 71, 102
fruits, 14, 43, 45, 84, 115, 121, 123, 128

gambling, 109, 111
  cockfighting, 109
  horse racing, 109

General Charles de Gaulle, 36
government, 33–39

harbor facilities, 11
Hawaii, 7–17, 46–49, 87–93
health care, 70–71
  hospitals, 12, 70
history, 19–31
housing, 69–70

immigration, 35, 59, 63, 64
income, 12, 13, 28, 30, 41, 42, 43, 67, 68, 73, 108
independence, 19, 29, 30, 31, 33, 36, 38, 68, 69
industrial development, 51
infrastructure, 57
investment, 42

justice, 12, 35

King Pomare I, 26
King Pomare II, 24, 26, 77, 78, 79, 82

labor force, 73
landowners, 21, 22, 61, 68, 69
languages, 87–93
  French, 89–90
  Tahitian, 87–93, 102
Law of the Sea, 47
legislative power, 34
leisure, 105–111
  bringue, 111, 116, 121, 128
life expectancy, 59
literature, 19, 71, 101–102
local government, 37

Mahaena, 27, 45
Mahina, 11, 13, 59, 80
maps
  cultural Tahiti, 136
  economic Tahiti, 134
  map of Tahiti, 132
Mataiea, 43, 82, 102
Matavai Bay, 10, 16
men, 25, 27, 34, 48, 64, 65, 75, 84, 95, 96, 98, 99, 100, 106, 110, 113, 114
military, 26, 30, 34, 36, 38, 39, 42, 43, 55, 64, 70, 73, 115, 116
mineral deposits, 47

missionaries, 11, 24, 26, 27, 65, 75, 77, 78, 80, 83, 89, 97, 103, 117
modern technology, 43
Moorea, 7, 11, 28, 34, 48, 51, 57
mountains, 7, 10, 13
    Mount Diademe, 11
    Mount Orohena, 10, 13
    Mount Roniu, 10
municipal councils, 37
museums, 12, 102

national flower, 14, 15, 113, 118
nationalism, 36
National Marine Research Center, 47
newspapers, 90–91
New Zealand, 7, 38, 39, 45, 46, 87
nuclear program, 30, 39
nuclear tests, 29, 30, 36, 38, 39, 41, 54, 55, 57, 79

offices, 12, 42, 117

Pacific Ocean, 7, 7–17
Paea, 11, 13, 80
painter
    Gauguin, Paul, 102
Papara, 8, 11, 43, 45
Papeari, 43, 54, 102
Papeete, 8, 10, 11, 12, 13, 36, 37, 38, 41, 42, 44, 46, 49, 56, 59, 63, 67, 69, 70, 71, 72, 73, 75, 80, 81, 90, 93, 96, 101, 102, 103, 108, 114, 115, 116, 117, 118, 119, 121, 123, 128, 129
Papeete Market, 128–129
parliament, 30, 34
patchwork quilt, 103
pearls, 44, 46
Pirae, 8, 13, 38, 49, 59, 70, 108
police, 35, 37, 43
population, 7, 13, 19, 24, 27, 31, 35, 36, 38, 51, 52, 53, 55, 56, 57, 59, 61, 62, 64, 68, 69, 77, 78, 79, 80, 91, 113, 121
Pouvanaa Committee, 29, 36
poverty, 63, 67, 69, 102
president, 31, 33, 34, 38, 39, 114
protectorate, 26, 27, 28, 78, 80

Punaauia, 13, 14, 81, 117

Queen Pomare IV, 26, 78, 80

radio and television, 91, 93
Raiatea, 7, 19, 48, 59
recipes
    firifiri, 131
    raw fish salad, 130
religion, 77–85
    ancient beliefs and pagan worship, 84–85
    Christianity, 77, 79
        Catholicism, 77, 80–81
        Protestantism, 12, 26, 77, 78–79, 82, 117
rivers, 11, 17, 57, 107
    Papeete, 11
    Papenoo, 11, 14
    Vaitepiha, 11

schools, 8, 12, 63, 72, 77, 79, 81, 83, 87, 96, 108
security, 33, 42
socializing, 105
social problems, 67, 73–74
social structure, 67–69
South America, 21
sports, 108
    basketball, 108
    cockfighting, 108
    French bowling, 108
    golf, 108
    horseback riding, 108
    soccer, 108
    tennis, 108
    volleyball, 108

Tahitian drums, 110
Tahitian flag, 33
Tahitian names, 92
Tahitians, 59–65
Tahiti Iti, 8, 10, 51
Tahiti Nui, 8, 10, 11, 35, 51, 93
Taravao, 8, 43, 80
taxes, 41
Teva I Uta, 43
theater, 102

Tiarei, 8, 45
tourism, 44, 46–48, 51, 57, 64, 69, 87, 91
trade, 45–46
    exports, 11, 45, 46
    imports, 45
trading partners, 46
traditional dress, 64–65
    pareu, 64, 65, 97, 98, 108
transportation, 49
    minibuses, 49
tribes, 23
Tuauru, 16

unemployment, 30, 41, 42, 67, 73
United Nations, 33, 47
United States, 29, 46, 83, 128

valleys, 11, 14
vanilla, 14, 45, 63, 128
volcanic islands, 7
volcanoes, 8, 9, 10

wages, 31
wars
    American Civil War, 62
    World War I, 29, 36
    World War II, 29, 55, 63, 96
water activities, 107
    stone fishing, 110, 111
weddings, 111
women, 22, 56, 64, 65, 73, 74, 75, 80, 83, 84, 95, 97, 98, 99, 100, 103, 106, 110, 114, 119, 125, 127
    vahine, 64, 74, 75, 89, 101, 102
World Trade Organization, 42
World Wildlife Fund (WWF), 51
writers
    Brooke, Rupert, 101
    Loti, Pierre, 91, 101
    Melville, Herman, 101